RICHARD WAGAMESE SELECTED

RICHARD WAGAMESE SELECTED

WHAT COMES FROM SPIRIT

with an introduction by
DREW HAYDEN TAYLOR

Douglas & McIntyre

FOR EACH COPY of this book sold, the publisher will make a donation to the Ontario Arts Foundation in support of the Indigenous Voices Awards: indigenousvoicesawards.org

TEXT COPYRIGHT © 2021 ESTATE OF RICHARD ALLEN WAGAMESE GILKINSON
INTRODUCTION COPYRIGHT © 2021 DREW HAYDEN TAYLOR
1 2 3 4 5 — 25 24 23 22 21

DOUGLAS AND MCINTYRE (2013) LTD.
P.O. Box 219, Madeira Park, BC, VON 2HO
www.douglas-mcintyre.com

FRONT COVER IMAGE: Thompson River by Chris Harris, All Canada Photos
COVER DESIGN by Diane Robertson
TEXT DESIGN by Shed Simas / Onça Design
PRINTED AND BOUND in Canada
PRINTED on 100% recycled paper

DOUGLAS AND MCINTYRE acknowledges the support of the Canada Council for the Arts, the Government of Canada, and the Province of British Columbia through the BC Arts Council.

LIBRARY AND ARCHIVES CANADA CATALOGUING IN PUBLICATION
Title: Richard Wagamese selected : what comes from spirit.
Other titles: Works. Selections | What comes from spirit
Names: Wagamese, Richard, author. | Taylor, Drew Hayden, 1962- writer of introduction.
Description: Introduction by Drew Hayden Taylor. | Includes bibliographical references.
Identifiers: Canadiana (print) 2021025484X | Canadiana (ebook) 20210254866 |
    ISBN 9781771622752 (hardcover) | ISBN 9781771622769 (EPUB)
Subjects: LCGFT: Essays. | LCGFT: Creative nonfiction.
Classification: LCC PS8595.A363 A6 2021 | DDC C818/.5408—dc23

CONTENTS

INTRODUCTION

DREW HAYDEN TAYLOR

"I've come to understand that the pain of a wound or a loss is over as soon as it happens. What follows is the pain of getting well."
—RICHARD WAGAMESE

ANOTHER RICHARD WAGAMESE BOOK for the public to enjoy. The literary gods indeed must be feeling benevolent.

In the Canadian literary landscape, there exists what is known as The Two Margarets: Laurence and Atwood. Two phenomenal writers who, it can safely be said, had a hand in the development of contemporary Canadian literature. You say "The Two Margarets," and if you can't immediately name them and some of their works . . . well, it's time to hand in your citizenship.

In the Indigenous literary universe, the same can be said about The Two Richards: Wagamese and Van Camp. Anybody familiar with the stories coming from our communities will know those names. If not, time to hand in your Status card. And also, I guess, your citizenship as well.

But it is perhaps Richard Wagamese who has captured the Canadian zeitgeist best of all us Indigenous writers. His prolific outpouring of quality storytelling and his unfortunate death have cemented him quite firmly in what I (and to my knowledge nobody else) refer to as the Contemporary Indigenous Literary

Renaissance. Novels, poetry, non-fiction . . . he was a master of them all. If his name was attached to it, you knew there was substance behind it. He was an amazing writer, and more importantly, an amazing man. His smile was as bright as his craft.

He was also one of those rare writers who always had something pertinent to say. That comes, possibly, from living such a complex life. Part of the infamous Sixties Scoop, Richard had a lot of life experience with the trials and tribulations of being an Indigenous youth in Canada to draw upon for his work. Add to that his eventual return to his family, people and culture, and there was enough experience instilled in him for several lifetimes.

A thousand years ago when I was taking my first infant steps as a literary storyteller, I wondered if I was doing the right thing. I had stories to tell but I didn't know if I should be doing that. Back then, there weren't a lot of us around and job opportunities for us First Nations dudes (writers notwithstanding) were limited: fishing guide, heavy equipment operator, steel worker and perhaps an actor on *The Beachcombers*.

Then I happened upon a traditional storyteller just north of Manitoulin Island who took me aside and told me, quite emphatically, "We need the new stories as much as we need the old stories." And that is how I have always perceived Richard: a contemporary storyteller. A word warrior if you must, telling his stories to the world. His words helped the dominant culture to understand this generation of Indigenous people. They also helped us, I mean those same Indigenous people, to comprehend and appreciate the power of two things: the human mind and a keyboard. Together, those two things can make all things possible.

Richard's magical tales, in whatever form, had that power to change the world. And they did. The number of people whom I have come across who have been personally moved by his words . . . well, that would fill up a book in itself. His readers feel his pain and his joy, his confusion and his understanding. And they come away the better for it.

Case in point: this collection of writings in particular. They are an assemblage of his thoughts, short pieces, and in some cases, brief reflections gathered from social media. Idle thoughts that Richard shared with the world. Gathered from his blog, newspaper columns and Facebook account, there are over two decades of topics that Richard pondered about. In these pages, you will see his wanderings, his philosophy, his searching and his delight at what the latter half of his life had provided for him and how it reflected on his first half. There could be no better window into the soul of the man behind such books as *Indian Horse*, *Medicine Walk* and *One Native Life*.

Stories, and I speak as a writer, have a soul. They have a spirit. They have a life—at least, the good ones do. This is true for all works of art. They should have their creators' DNA in them. So, you know when you've come across a Wagamese original. Sometimes cruel and critical, other times light and life-affirming, his musings will take you to so many unexpected places.

As an artist, Richard always made his past front and centre in his writings. Whether those experiences were good or bad, they flavoured everything he worked on. The man wrote about what had happened in his young and not-so-young life, whether directly or hidden behind the curtains of prose fiction. And his departure from this earth frequently makes us wonder where his writings would have led us in the future. In recognition of the mentorship Richard showed to emerging writers, part of the publisher's proceeds from this book will be given to the Indigenous Voices Awards to support the next generation of Indigenous literary talent.

If those same literary gods were kinder, I would have personally loved to have sat down with Richard and whiled away endless hours talking novel . . . talking biography . . . talking simple storytelling. Now, that would have been an honour. But alas, other than a few occasional encounters, we never had that chance. This book is perhaps the closest I will get to doing that. Most of his novels exist in a universe he created for us, but here is the universe Richard Wagamese lived in.

If you are holding this book in your hands, you are obviously a devotee. It's hard not to be. Treasure these timeless words. Honour his thoughts. But don't read it too fast. Soak it in. Enjoy every morsel. Linger on each page because every paragraph has nuggets of understanding. Lines of wisdom. Stories to appreciate.

I know of what I speak, for I am talking to you as one fan to another.

DREW HAYDEN TAYLOR
Curve Lake, Ontario
July 2021

I

THE LAND IS
A FEELING

STORIES BEGAN IN A CAVE

THERE'S A CAVE in a rock cliff in northern Ontario. It lies somewhere just north of the town line of Kenora. Although I haven't been there in years, lately I've been returning there in my mind because that was where everything really started.

I used to run away. Whenever life in my foster home would get too rough I disappeared there. I'd discovered it one summer day while exploring the woods. The cave was a small opening in the cliff, hidden from view by a pair of tall, bushy pine trees. Over time I'd managed to stash cookies, blankets, candles, flashlights and pen and paper there. It became my refuge.

Whenever I'd disappear, the police would comb Kenora looking for me. Meanwhile I would be safely ensconced in my little hideaway perched some five metres off the ground watching the wind blow through the tops of the pine forest.

The foster-home situation was a frightening and strange experience. People I barely knew were forcing new attitudes, rules and regulations on me and I was scared. I remembered my life with my natural family. This new experience was unsettling since no one had ever bothered to explain the rationale to me. The little cave in the woods was the only place I knew that made sense and where there was no fear.

I'd been born in a trapline tent in the middle of the bush so the sights and sounds of the rough and tangle were always more of a comfort than a threat. In that cave there was never anyone to please: no one to pacify by adopting strange new behaviours and no one to placate by being anything other than what I was.

In that cave I could be myself and dream whatever dreams arose. There was pen and paper so I could write them down. I'd light candles, munch cookies and write stories about the life I recalled on the trapline. I'd write happy tales of long evenings spent with my mother and father, of birthday parties and camping trips, fishing and hunting. I'd write everything the way I wished my life was really like. When the cold and the discomfort and hunger got to be too much I'd sadly sneak back into town.

In that little cave the desire to write was born. Writing became an escape from the foster home. Through poems and stories I lived the lives of kids who never have to disappear, whose family is never taken away and whose future is bright, predictable and free of caves.

One day at school they asked us what we hoped to be when we grew up. My classmates responded with the traditional roll call of fireman, policeman, the odd cowboy, father, mother and circus performer. When my turn came I whispered shyly, "I want to make stories."

Make stories. Back then I didn't realize that the cultural history and development of my people was perpetuated through stories and legend. I didn't realize that a big part of who I was, and am, was possible because old men and women would sit around a tribal fire in the long winter nights and spin tales of mystery that spoke of the heartbeat of a people who called themselves *Anishinaabeg*. The Ojibway. I just knew how right it felt to make stories in that small cave in the woods.

As the years went by—thirty some by now—I never ever forgot those nights alone in the ink of a northern night writing and reading by flashlight, never forgot the calm and strength that came from the process of going inward to create outward. Fortunately, I've been able to evolve into a maker of stories who gets paid regularly for doing openly what I had to hide to do as a child. Making stories. There's room in Native circles for story-makers. Just as there's room for painters, singers, dancers, hunters, leaders and craftspeople. I learned that from the Old One who told me point-blank that makers of stories are vital to the people and to keep going. And I have.

THE LAND IS A FEELING. Sitting beside the fire in this winsome river valley, the mountains seem to enfold you as deeply as the night. Against the sky they become a single purple smudge atop the shadowed apex of pine and poplar.

The river gurgle snakes through the sharp crackle of the fire just long enough to remind you where the real power lies. It's a feeling I've come to recognize as *home*.

SUNLIGHT SPILLS OVER the
mountain like a newfound joy. There
is the sparkle for the symphony
of the sky all glassine, blue and
shimmering on the placid face
of the lake. Birdsong. Life energy.
reawakening all around you.

PURPLE WORLD

WHEN THE SUN SETS behind these mountains you can almost see them begin to breathe. It's a trick of the light, really, something created by the encroaching purple darkness, distance and an indefinable desire for magic.

The Old Ones believed that this was a strong spirit time. The grandfathers and grandmothers whose spirits reside within these trees, rocks, rivers and mountains would come alive again and around those ancient tribal fires their songs would be sung, and the drums would echo the heartbeat of the universe to welcome them.

My *mishomis*, Ojibway for grandfather, described this time and the mountains breathing as the universe giving a collective shrug. It was his way of saying that the Earth is alive.

[. . .]

In the Indian way of seeing, the land, and all things that move upon it, is alive and therefore sacred. Humankind's relationship to the Earth and its life forms has always been that of an equal. The honour of one is the honour of all. If you cared enough to consider the guardianship of yourself and your family, it followed that you cared enough to consider the guardianship of the Earth.

[. . .]

What it takes is a walk upon the land. Learning to see these things that exist here with something other than your eyes. Leaving the material trappings behind awhile and allowing yourself to become part of the sweep and grandeur of the planet: allowing your heartbeat.

When you do that, you learn to see the mountains, begin to breathe in the falling darkness. You learn to accept the responsibility that comes with being a part of Creation and you begin to understand, as the Old Ones understand, that the honour of one thing is the honour of all.

YOU HAVE TO REALLY SEE the morning to come to believe in it. Not a dawn groggy with little sleep or a mind already busy sorting through obligations or rushing about preparing for another hectic frenzy but a morning full of deep silence and an absolute clarity of perception. A dawn you observe around you degree by degree.

WOOD DUCKS

THERE ARE BIRDS on the water. There are red wing blackbirds, and bluish swallows that dart and wheel crazily in the hard slice of the sun between mountains. Against the treed rim of the far shore, loons offer their wobbly cries. In the reeds there's a thin grey poke of heron, mute and patient, and a pair of Canada Geese behind him.

It's spring now, the turn of it out of winter slow and lazy, like the land is a bear, sluggish from sleep and unconvinced about motion. There's a peacefulness to it that fills me. There's something in this ballet of motion that kindles in me a fire that first burned a long, long time ago. A tribal fire, even though at first, I didn't recognize it as that.

I was eleven. I'd moved three times in the two years I'd been with my adopted family. I'd been in three schools, lived in three houses, learned to form friendships and lose them three separate times. We were settled in a rented farmhouse on three hundred acres in Bruce County in southwestern Ontario. I ached for permanence.

That first fall and winter I discovered the maple bush in the back forty. I went there to watch the colours change, to sit in the high branches of a big, old maple and see the gold, scarlet and orange emerge against the hard punch of blue through the branches.

When spring came the land was sogged with mud. I waited eagerly so I could get away and wander. I'd found a peacefulness there that filled me and I craved the solitude and the feel of the land around me. Being on the land had eased my fears and it was only there that I felt truly alive and free.

Finally, I was out. I saw woodchuck and fox kits, fawns, calves, and in the trees, the nesting activities of birds. I extended my range to the marsh that reached back from the old dam near the highway and flooded a low lying section of bush.

The water was about a foot and a half deep. With my gumboots on I could wander anywhere in that bayou-like stillness. There were muskrats there, water snakes and swimming creatures of all varieties crossing the marsh on their rounds. I learned to walk without disturbing the water, to sneak through the shadow silently, and that's how I discovered the wood ducks.

They were the most beautiful creatures I had ever seen. The male was all green and purple, deep red, yellow and black. The female was a demure grey with white at her throat and bluish wings. When I first saw them they were sitting on a half submerged log and I stopped and stood stock still in the water. They swam within feet of me and I marveled at them.

They had a nest in the crotch of a rotted tree stump three feet off the water. I climbed a tree about ten yards away and looked down into it. There were eight eggs there and they were as beautiful as the parents, all tan and cream and quiet, and as I stood in that tree watching them I almost felt I could see them move, breathe in that opaque stillness.

I went back to that tree every day to watch those eggs and wait for them to hatch. They knew I was there but I was quiet and non-threatening and they came to accept me. I sat in that neighboring tree and kept vigil over those eggs.

Something happened to me there. Braced in a tree above a flooded bush, peering through shadow and hardly breathing, I came to fully occupy the space I was in for the very first time in my life. There was no need for things and stuff, no need of other people, no need for anything but that nest of eggs, the boggy smell of that place and the feeling that I only know today as perfection.

I watched those eight wood duck chicks hatch. They emerged one day in the late afternoon and I saw all of it. Days later I saw them drop the three feet to the water and begin to swim with their parents, as pure and natural as breathing. When I left them for the last time I didn't feel the sense of departure I'd learned so well in my life. Instead, I felt joined to them.

Some things in life remain. Some things transcend the losses and leavings of our living. I found the essence of my tribal self in that tree above the nest and it never left me. When the time was right and I was ready, I emerged as a tribal person, as pure and natural as breathing.

TEACHINGS ARE HIDDEN in every leaf and rock.

GRANDFATHER'S GIFT

THIS IS THE FAMILY TIME.

The Ojibway call it Long Snows Moon.

In traditional times, the moons of winter were seen as teaching moons.

The Elders would sit beside the tribal fires and tell the old stories. The people would gather their families and clans to listen to these magical tales that taught as much as they entertained.

The family was the centre of tribal life.

Children were treated with as much respect as their Elders, and their education was conducted by every member of the band.

The extended-family concept was understood and practised by the Indians for many generations prior to the arrival of the white man.

[...]

[My grandfather] John Wagamese was a man of the bush.

He was a northern Ontario Ojibwa who never learned the English language. Nor did he learn any work other than that involved in the lifestyle of a traditional Ojibwa. He hunted, fished and trapped. He spent his entire life in close contact with the bush and the way of life that sustained and defined him.

I was born on the trapline in the fall of 1955.

For the first two years of my life I lived in the bush with my two brothers, a sister, mother and father, grandmother and grandfather. It was a happy time.

The Ontario Hydro Corp. decided they really needed to build a dam or two on the Winnipeg River, close to where we were living.

The resulting flood forced my family to abandon their traditional lifestyle and move to town. Soon after, my brothers and sister and I found ourselves in the foster-care system.

Not long after this, I disappeared.

I would not see my family again for twenty years.

The Children's Aid Society, in their infinite wisdom, saw fit to separate me from my family. I wound up living in the suburbs of Toronto. By some miracle, my oldest brother located me when I was twenty-two and serving time in an Ontario jail.

He provided a home for me and it wasn't long before I was reunited with the family I barely remembered.

It wasn't long before I was prowling the northern Ontario bush that had brought me such happiness as a young boy. This is where the story lives.

As I spent more and more time reuniting myself with the bush, I noticed something strange. Somehow in my wanderings I could see things. I somehow knew the bear signs, the deer signs, the holes in the waters where the pickerel lay, the names of plants and their uses. After twenty years, I knew this bush as though I'd never left it.

I asked my grandfather. We had to speak through an interpreter because I'd lost my traditional tongue by then. Our conversations were long and often difficult because Ojibwa doesn't translate easily into English. But he understood.

What he told me still ranks as the greatest gift I have ever received. He told me that the reason I knew these things was because he had made sure I was introduced to them very early.

Whenever he would head into the bush during the first two years of my life, he would bundle me up in my cradle-board and strap me to his chest. As he walked through the bush he would talk to me and tell me about the things we passed.

If we encountered a bear or a deer, he would tell me its traditional name and about its ways.

He would stop and talk to me about the plants we found. He would tell me about the winds and how to use them as a method of finding my way.

He told me about everything that we encountered in our travels.

This was the traditional way, he said. A grandfather or father would take a young Ojibwa child out into the world and introduce him or her to it all.

My grandfather told me that he took this time with me because he wanted to make sure that when I was old enough to explore the world on my own, I wouldn't feel like a stranger.

This is the way of the Indians. Giving to the children is the natural process.

Passing on insights, knowledge and ways of seeing were and are integral to child rearing in Indian circles.

In these modern times there is much to be learned from this. At this time of the year it is good to recall. The spirit of giving to children goes far beyond the gifts, the wrapping, the joy and spirit of one particular morning.

It's a process and a way of being.

THERE'S A SMALL, weathered hand drum that graces my living room wall. It's made from the skin of a moose and its frame is made from the trunk of a tree. Circular in shape to reflect the circle of life, it was given to me by the Old Man who helped connect me to my inner reality and who helped me relate it to everything around me.

The drum represents the heartbeat of the people. When we were babies in our mother's womb we were comforted by her heartbeats. As we moved out into the world the Creator granted us the drum to remind us that the Earth too, is our mother.

Because of that we are to respect, honour and protect her just as we would our human mother.

Whenever the drum is heard, it serves as a reminder to Aboriginal people of the special relationship they have with the land. It's a comforting sound because it stirs that special something inside us that recalls our mother's heartbeat. That unique place that exists within, around, and upon the land.

WHERE THE HEART IS

MY ELDERS SAY that we dream ourselves into being. That sounds powerfully esoteric but it isn't nearly as hard to decipher as you might think. It simply means we have the ability to become whomever we choose to become. All of us. There's no limit to our human potential and there's no limit to where our spirits can choose to go. Hot on the heels of the power of choice is the power of allowing. We Ojibway have a phrase for that—*yuh-gotta-wanna*.

For me, the great fact is that I would be Ojibway wherever I went. It's just here in this idyllic setting where I choose to express myself and where I allow magic to happen. Within me are the legends and teachings and philosophy of my people and I carry them proudly. Not a day goes by that I am not thankful for the guidance of those things nor a day when they do not affect the way I travel through that day.

I've walked the shores of the Winnipeg River. I've visited sacred sites and ceremonial places. I've trekked to the remote sites where my family camped to trap and fish when I was born. That territory marked me and it is special to me. To go there is to feel a connection I have never found an appropriate word for in English. To say it is spiritual somehow reduces it. It's spiritual, emotional, mental and physical all at the same time.

I don't know whether I really get homesick. The way my life went, I was in and out of a lot of homes as a kid and teenager. As a young adult I never really felt at home until I came here. I do get lonesome for the land though. Stuck in cities as I was for so many years I felt a melancholy I never could figure out. Once I walked out into the bush again or stood at the edge of a northern lake I understood what it was I'd been missing.

We dream ourselves. I dream of those things and those places where my life began. Sometimes I see myself walking there. Sometimes I see myself surrounded by people I never got a chance to know. But I always awake to the silence of our home in the mountains and I am always grateful to be here. There is no other place for me.

Within each of us is the residue of the places we come from. We carry the information of our cultures and our histories within us like latent genes.

When we move, when we choose to live somewhere other than our traditional homes, those are the things that allow us to dream ourselves into fullness. Our touchstones. The feel of home we carry between our ribs. It's not an Ojibway thing. It's a human one.

WHAT REMAINS THE SAME

WHEN YOU COME to stand upon the land there's a sense in you that you've seen it all before. Not in any empirical way perhaps. Not in any western sense of recognition. But more in the way it comes to feel upon your skin, the way it floods you with recollection.

Standing beside a tiny creek in the mountains I suddenly remember how it felt to catch minnows in a jar. The goggle-eyed sense of wonder at those silvered, wriggling beams of light darting between stones and the feel of the water on my arms, cool and slick as the surface of dreams.

I lived my life for the sudden flare of sunlight when I broke from the bush back then. The land beckoned through my bedroom window so that sometimes when the house was quiet I stood there just to hear the call of it spoken in a language that I didn't know. Calling me to it.

That creek ran out of farmland and wound its way to the reservoir behind an old mill, the voice of it a chuckle, its edges dappled by the shadows of old elms and its light like the dancing bluish green eyes of the girl on the bus you could never find a way to say a word to.

I'd lay across a long flat stone to dip a mason jar elbows deep and hung there, suspended, while minnows nibbled at my fingertips. I let that arm dangle until the feeling went away then raised it with minnows frantic in the sudden absence of their world.

I couldn't keep them. Couldn't carry them home like a carnival prize, give them names or place them in a bowl upon my desk. No, something in me understood that some things ache to be free and the charm of them resides in their ability to be that freedom.

So I let them go. Let them swim away. But I carried something of that creek, that cold against my arms, the sun-warmed stone against my belly, the breeze, the light and the idea of minnows away with me forever.

So that standing on the edge of another creek at fifty-five it's like years haven't happened at all. It's a journey, this life. A crossing of creeks on stepping stones where so much comes to depend on maintaining balance on every careful placing of the foot.

SNOW SPIRALS OUT of grey tucked in at the edge of mountains and it's so quiet now you can hear them sigh to Earth. You lean on the shovel and wonder how things can seem so empty and so full all at one time . . . but thankful that they can.

THE ONLY EXTRAORDINARY THING I've done is to never allow the mistakes of my past to discolour or erode my hope for the future. Because it's not the big things that add up in the end; it's the hundreds, thousands, millions of little things we do on a regular basis that define our lives as extraordinary, like teaching someone to love the taste of cold blueberries or how to find a planet in the night sky or how perfectly a Brahms sonata fits a rainy morning . . . those are the extraordinary things that define a life.

TRUE SILENCE IS MORE than just not talking. It's responding to that deep inner yearning I carry to feel myself alive, to exist beyond my thinking, to live beyond worry and frustration. True silence is calm being. True silence is appreciating the moment for the moment. Every breath a connection to my life force, my essence. It is the grandest music I have ever heard.

WOLF TRACKS

THERE WERE WOLF TRACKS on the gravel road. In the mountains where we live that shouldn't be odd. But it is. I can only recall seeing a wolf once before in four years so the tracks surprised me.

Standing at the side of the road while the dog snooped about at the strange scent I felt the aura of wildness all around me. It was powerful and brought with it whirls of ideas and shards of knowledge. Wolves are creatures of mystery. They are beasties of the full moon and long shadow.

They're part of our own primordial past, a link to that time when we were bands of wanderers, all of us, seeking shelter in fire, in community, in each other. The tracks angled off into the trees eventually but the wolf's presence was palpable and exciting.

Returning to my workspace, switching on the computer, and checking emails it occurred to me how easily we create distance between ourselves and that world. Steps away from the head of the driveway, a wolf lurked. But instantaneously I'm in cyberspace and galaxies away from that connection. It was a jarring realization.

As a Native person whose ceremonial and spiritual sense comes from a relationship with the land, I don't feel comfortable knowing I can shut it off like a light switch. As a human being with stewardship obligations to the planet that's my home, I'm embarrassed. As a writer often expressing themes of kinship I'm stunned by it.

Maybe there's something bigger in a wolf track than anomaly. Maybe there are teachings in things, like my people say, meant to draw us back into relationship, to our kinship with the planet. Or, perhaps, jolts of wild are necessary conduits to a reordering of how we spend our time here, reminders that we are animals too and we need to form a pack and help each other.

I don't know. All I know for sure, is that something as simple as a wolf track in the mud of a burgeoning summer is enough to confound me.

That's what's worth holding—that palpable mystery. That charge in the belly that says "we are not alone" and "you cannot order everything." The planet is not here for us. Rather, we are here for the planet. Something as simple as a wolf track can take us back to that.

RAIN FALLS HEAVY as a curtain and everywhere there is the sound of applause on the streets where everyday people aim themselves at their lives in deliberate trajectories and no one notices the world's ovation or the hands of the rain dripping off the brim of a hat, gentle on their faces. This a poem this world, this life, this elegant morning bathed in the tears Mother Earth sheds to cleanse us, everything.

THERE'S MAGIC IN THE SOUND

of a human voice augmented by the crackle of a fire. There's something ancient and eternal that stirs things within us and you don't have to be a native person to understand that. Everyone from every culture has a fire and a story in their past.

BEYOND THIS CITY'S JUT and angle there is a bend in the river with a slab of rock set against the rushing current of a river sluicing through a filigree of cliff and tree and sky. Meet me there. We'll sit on that rock, open our hearts and listen and not say a word, merely gaze at what is real and pure and perfect. When we allow our souls to inhabit such places the world becomes too full to talk about and we carry that silence home.

DARK TO LIGHT

WHEN FRIENDS FROM THE CITY come to our home in the mountains they are always amazed at how dark it gets. After they're awed by the power of the sunsets up here where the air is clear of smog and grit, they settle into a kind of eerie silence.

It's like you can feel the idea of approaching night on the open land pulling at them, taking them back to a primordial memory of being one of a band of hunters huddled around a fire for protection against the noises in the night.

Then, as the sky turns deep blue, then purple and the stars wink into view and a slip of moon rises over the trees, the darkness falls like an eyelid on the world. That's when they get real quiet. That's when you can feel the wonder, the awe, the sheer amazement at the power of a rural darkness.

When there is no moon the quality of darkness here is absolute. When there's only a slice of moon the world exists in shadow and stretches of blue white light. Sometimes, when the moon is full the darkness becomes a puzzle to be solved with the eyes.

We forget all that when we live in cities. There we live in a strange orange or yellow glow at night. We live bathed in neon. Light is the absolute and darkness is relegated to those places the light won't reach and we don't learn it at all.

There's an ancient magic to whole darkness. It's the magic of shamans, seers and healers. It's the magic that transforms us. We confront a power that is beyond our ability to negotiate with, to control, to change, alter, or arrange to suit us. It brings us to the realization of our proper size.

Darkness is where we meet our secrets. It's where we confront our fears. It's where our trolls and ogres and witches and beasties exist and we remember how small a species we really are. After a lifetime in the city darkness on the land reminds us all of that.

I like to watch how it affects them. I like to watch them go quiet. I like to watch them huddle closer to the fire. Because I know when the light returns, when morning breaks, they will emerge into it with a bigger idea of their place in the world and who they were created to be.

II

THE TRUTH STAYS THE SAME

NEVER FORGET THAT we carry a common practical magic within us; that we are star dust and we carry comets and whirlwinds inside of us. That we are all magical beings—and we always were.

I AM DRAWN to ceremony like Earth is drawn in its circle around the sun. To begin a day's journey without a smudge, a prayer and meditation is to lack a centre. I'm not a holy man or a great ceremonialist. I only know that ceremony is the magnet that draws me closer to Creator, to the Grandmothers, to my essential and truest self. It doesn't have to be elaborate. Breathing is a ceremony when it's mindful. So is walking. So is looking at something that moves me. So is talking when the talk is real and earnest.

THERE ARE NO STRANGERS.
The same North Star guides us
all home.

LEARNING VITAL LESSONS: INFLATING FROGS

WE INFLATED FROGS.

Young and reckless and full of the joys of unrestrained energies by boys the world over. Indian boys. Our world at that time was the rough and tangle of the northern Ontario bush.

It was ours. Every day in climbing, creeping, running and walking through it we became as familiar with its motions and stillness as we were with our playground, our chapel and to a certain degree our teacher.

But we inflated frogs.

We'd head out in droves every springtime. The rivers would be alive with swarms of pickerel on their spawning runs. Simply catching the largest fish of the season was enough to elevate a boy right up into the very stuff of legend. Competition was fierce.

We'd insert a milkshake straw into an appropriate orifice and inflate the frog.

Someone had discovered that an adequately inflated frog would thrash wildly along the surface of the water. The pickerel, of course, would go crazy. We could locate the hole where the big fish lay by the churn and gulp of water as the frog disappeared.

Back then I didn't know.

I didn't know that the frog's life, as with all life, was sacred. I didn't know that because of this it should be respected. I didn't know the vital difference between ingenuity and disregard just as I didn't know that what I was doing was wrong.

Because I had no one to teach me and I did not understand.

The progression of my life found me on the street at seventeen. After a decade and a half within the relative security of the foster-care system, I was woefully unprepared.

Suddenly, I was seen as just another crazy, shiftless, dirty Indian. No one had told me that these attitudes existed. No one had told me that in the eyes of many I would be pre-judged, pre-destined and pre-labelled.

I reacted badly. Soon enough I found myself in the company of other young Indians. They were angry. They were filled with resentment and hatred for four hundred years of abuse and betrayal.

And so I learned to glare into the face of white society and overtly demand rights I barely understood.

Back then I didn't know.

I didn't know that history can't be changed. I didn't know that anger is an all-consuming thing. I didn't know that balance and harmony with all things is the Indian way. Most of all, I didn't know that the creed of the warrior included compassion, respect, honour and kindness just as I didn't know that warriors were allowed to cry.

Because I had no one to teach me and I did not understand.

The years have changed me. When I began to sit with the Elders of my people and listen to the ancient teachings and values, I began to learn to see. I began to see that this circle of people of which I was a part were much more than the images I'd had presented to me all my life. I began to see the people. I began to learn.

Many people come to me in the course of my daily travels and ask me certain things. One of the most common concerns is the reason Canada's Native people are always making such a fuss.

To the untrained eye it might seem that things are reasonably okay out there in Indian country. To those same untrained eyes it might seem that all this political hullaballoo is bothersome and unnecessary.

Because they had no one to teach them and they do not understand.

The answer quite simply is this. In every Indian community, on every reserve, the Elders who possess that old, traditional knowledge are dying.

It's this knowledge that Indian people are fighting to preserve. At the bottom of every political confrontation, litigation and news release lies the overriding concern for the preservation of that cultural way.

Because those cultural values and spiritual ways have been what has enabled the Indians to survive the enormous changes they've endured in so short a time.

And it's what will enable them to survive in the future.

[. . .]

It's important, vitally important, that these old ways and teachings be continued. They are what define and sustain us as Indian people. Because the saddest image I carry in my mind is that of the last surviving Indian being asked why it is that he or she has no knowledge of the people and where they came from. And the response.

Because I had no one to teach me and I did not understand.

ME: What's the biggest strength Creator gives me?

OLD WOMAN: Choice.

ME: That seems kinda small.

OLD WOMAN: It's your true power. Your biggest power.

ME: Really? How so?

OLD WOMAN: With it you get to direct the course of your life. You can choose to give up. You can choose to hang on. You choose to feel angry. You choose to not listen, to stay tied to your past, to blame, to be prideful, to ignore humility. You choose your ego over your heart, to be a reactor or a creator. But you can also choose to let go, to have dignity, to forgive yourself and others, to see how valuable and beautiful you are, to be vulnerable and share your true self, to not be a victim. You can choose to be happy.

ME: All that is mine.

OLD WOMAN: It always was and always will be—but you have to choose to use it . . .

THE SYSTEM HAS A STAGGERING 374 FAULTS*

THERE'S AN OLD TATTOO on my forearm. Almost 20 years ago it came to symbolize my deep-seated sense of frustration with the justice system of Canada.

[. . .]

A cellmate carved the marijuana leaf into my arm with a pencil that was wound in thread and armed with a sewing needle as its tip. Ink was absorbed by the thread and planted under the skin with each sharp jab of the needle. I leaned against the barred door of our cell with my right arm thrust through the bars while my partner etched my rebellion permanently onto my person.

Homemade tattoos are taboo in prisons, so I "kept six" while the painful process was completed. Discovery would have put one or both of us in segregation, or as it's commonly referred to, "in the hole."

Not that I would have cared then. There wasn't anything more that the system could have done to me that hadn't already been

---

* This essay was originally published as a column in *The Calgary Herald* in 1991, in response to the release of "The Cawsey Report," which contained the findings of a task force on the criminal justice system and its impact on Indigenous people in Alberta. The "374 Faults" mentioned in the title references 374 failings of the justice system identified in the report.

done. I was back inside after serving previous time on a variety of offences. While inside I'd completed some high school courses, arranged to live on the reserve with my brother after my release, attended regular Narcotics and Alcoholics Anonymous meetings and talked about my problems with shrinks and social workers.

I was a perfect candidate for parole and when it was granted I felt positive about myself and my direction. The first day on the street I went to visit an old friend. We worked on his car as we talked. After a few hours I left to catch my bus to northern Ontario where my brother waited.

I'd forgotten about the wrench and screwdriver in my back pocket. It was nighttime and as I walked toward downtown a police cruiser slowed down to check me out. At that time I had almost waist-length hair that I kept tied with a red American Indian Movement headband, jeans, jean jacket and boots. They pulled me over immediately.

I identified myself as a parolee, specified my destination and when I was to report to my parole officer. I expected to be allowed to go. Instead the officers shone a flashlight in my eyes, asked me where I'd been drinking (I hadn't) and pushed me up against the cruiser for a frisk. When they discovered the forgotten tools they handcuffed me and took me downtown.

I was charged with possession of burglary tools. Believing it to be a mistake and not fully understanding the impact, in court the next day I admitted to having the tools. The officers referred to the high number of break-ins in the area where I was arrested and I was found guilty and sentenced to one year. I hadn't even bothered to get a lawyer since it all seemed so ridiculous.

Needless to say, my parole was revoked and I found myself facing another two years for, what seemed to me, an honest attempt to change. I believe today that, had I not been so obviously Native, it would never have happened.

I was angry. Once back in the institution a part of me gave up. I told my cellmate it was pointless to try to change because the system wasn't prepared to offer us the chance. A tattoo seemed like a good symbol of the rebellion within me. It was a few years before I would make another effort to turn my life around.

It took a Native Elder working with the system to reach the roots of my rebellion. It wasn't the system that helped me, but my own people and their traditions and teachings.

The justice system is failing Native people. That racism is a part of it all is implied firmly. It exists from the cop on the beat to the judge's chambers to the cellblock.

When thirty per cent of the prison population is comprised of one ethnic group something is terribly wrong.

Waiting on the government is no longer an option because there are far too many young writers, artists, scholars and leaders rotting away in the White man's jails; too many minds and bodies that are required to build a future; far too many fathers, mothers, sisters and brothers who are needed in their communities.

For their part, the government, police forces and courts need to develop the willingness to listen, really listen, to what Native groups are saying. And that, in the final analysis, is all the Indians have ever wanted.

WE WAKE TO A DAY of worry. But it's a time to remember that we are *Homo sapiens*. Translated literally to mean "wise man." And even though we have the greatest capacity for cruelty of any creature in Creation we also have the staunchest capacity for love, mercy, compassion, acceptance, forgiveness, empathy and kindness. We are built for survival because of those virtues. One man cannot change that. It will be a difficult time. But we were given knees on which to offer our humility to Creator and legs to stand strong in the face of adversity and hearts and minds and spirits wired for community. We have hands to reach out to one another. We have the inherent knowledge that we are one family. That is our saving grace.

THERE'S A PUZZLE I've been meaning to do. It's large and complicated. The longer I look at that complicated picture the less I'm willing to tackle the puzzle. So far it hasn't been done. Fortunately, life isn't a jigsaw puzzle. Life gives you the pieces but you get to choose the picture you want to create.

MOLE TALE MINES
SPIRITUAL DEPTH

A YOUNG MAN dreamed of being a great warrior. In his mind's eye he envisioned himself displaying tremendous bravery and earning the love and admiration of his people.

The young man knew that the greatest warriors were those who possessed the strongest spirits. He longed to become the greatest defender of his people.

When he reached the proper age he approached the Elder of his village. He told the Old One of his dream, of the great love and respect he felt within himself for his people and of his desire to protect them.

He asked the Old One to grant him the medicine power of the most respected animal in all of the animal kingdom. With this power the young man believed that he would be able to become as widely respected and feared as this animal brother.

The Old One smiled. Although he appreciated the young man's earnest desire he recognized that this was the time for a great teaching. So he told the young man that he would gladly grant him this medicine power if the youngster could accurately identify the animal who commanded the most respect from his animal brothers and sisters.

The young warrior smiled. It was obvious to him that the grizzly bear commanded the most respect in the animal world.

He stated this to his Elder and sat back awaiting the granting of the bear's medicine power.

The Old One smiled. He told the young man to guess again, for despite the immense courage and ferocity of the grizzly, there was one who commanded greater respect.

One by one the young man named the animals he felt possessed the adequate amount of fierceness, courage, boldness and fighting power to earn the awe of his four-legged brothers and sisters. He named the wolverine, the eagle, the cougar, the wolf and the bison, but each time the Old One simply smiled and told him to guess again.

Finally, in confusion, he surrendered.

The Elder told the young man he had guessed as wisely as he could. However not many knew the most respected of animals because the most respected one is seldom seen and even more seldom mentioned.

It is the tiny mole, the Old One said.

The tiny, sightless mole who lives within the earth. Because he is constantly in touch with Mother Earth, the mole is able to learn from her every day. Whenever some creature walked across the ground above him, the mole could feel its vibration in the earth. In order for the mole to know whether or not he was in danger he would always go to the surface to learn what created the vibration.

It is said by the Old People that the mole knows when the cougar is prowling above him just as he knows the approach of man and the scurry of the rabbit. Each time he sensed a vibration the mole crawled up to learn who was nearby.

And that is why the tiny mole is the animal among all animals who commands the greatest amount of respect. Because even though he might put himself at great danger, the mole always takes the time to investigate what he feels.

The young man understood. He rose to leave and thanked the Elder for the teaching. He was grateful that he had learned the true nature of the warrior and went on to become loved and respected as a brave, compassionate and respect warrior of his people.

This old story is still told to young Indian men as they approach maturity. At least it is still told by the Old Ones of my Ojibway people. It reflects in its simplicity the vast depth of spiritual insight that is at the heart and core of traditional Indian life. Then and now.

They called us pagans. As settlement of North America advanced, the settlers were fascinated by the array of seemingly heathen ritual. Everywhere there were nations of Indians sun-dancing, rain-dancing, corn-dancing, crawling into sweat lodges, chanting and burning strange forms of plant life. It was uncomfortable to souls accustomed to "established" religion.

It was assumed that the Indians had not had the benefit of any true spiritual teachings. Stories and legends were seen as charming little folk tales and little else.

There are virtually thousands of stories just like the mole story that exist across the length and breadth of North America. Within them are the traditional and cultural ethics, values and principles of a people who themselves were in constant contact with Mother Earth, and were thus able to learn from her every day. A people who have used those daily spiritual learnings to survive and develop despite tremendous changes in a short period of time.

I USED TO PRAY for everything I thought I wanted: big cars, big money, big and glittery everything. Mostly so I could feel glittery. That was always a struggle. These days I've learned to pray in gratitude for what's already here: prosperity, health, well-being, moments of joy and to pray for the same things for others. To paraphrase an old teaching, I'm learning to want nothing but to desire everything and to choose what appears. Life is easier that way, more graceful and I AM glittery—but from the inside out.

EAGLE FEATHERS

THERE ARE EAGLE FEATHERS that adorn our mountain home. They came to me through ceremony or acts of gratitude from people I worked with, or shared something special with. Each of them has a story and significance and I take pride in their presence in my home and my life. There is a pair from my wedding hung in my workspace. There are two hung above our entryway as a blessing for everyone who comes here. There is an eagle wing fan I use for prayer and ceremony.

They are beautiful things. What they represent to me is beautiful too although in the beginning I had a very limited idea of the teachings they carried. I understood that they represented honour and courage and a life lived on principle but I didn't know much else. For a time, getting an eagle feather was a huge focus in my life. I was under the assumption that to have one was to carry a stamp of approval, of belonging, of measuring up in the cultural scheme of things. I couldn't have been more wrong.

But I was as much a victim of misinformation as anybody, Native or non-native. Having grown up without my culture I relied on books, television, and movies to inform myself of what I mistook as genuine representation of myself. I saw great stoic and noble warriors wearing elaborate war bonnets or feathers hung from the back of their heads in battle and I believed that those feathers were all about fearlessness, courage and the whole "today is a good day to die" thing.

Then I had a conversation with an Elder friend when I was in my mid thirties. He was preparing some feathers for his powwow regalia and readying some to be given away at a ceremony we were attending. I told him about my fascination with the meaning of feathers to our people and he handed me one and asked me to look at it. I studied it for a while, ran my hand along its length, turned it over a time or two but I had no idea what he wanted me to see. When I gave it back to him he smiled and said there was a virtual university within that feather.

Look again, he said. As I studied it he told me where to look. He pointed to the spine and said that the spine that ran the length of it was the road of our life. It's thicker and fuller at the base and then gradually thins and softens and disappears eventually. Just like we do. In our early years we absorb learning. Our hearts and minds and spirits drink in everything. But as we grow we tend to forget our reliance on innocence and trust and humility. We become more concerned with practical things. But the teachings are always with us. In that it represents our life's journey.

Along both sides of that spine are hundreds of fine filaments that together make up the body of the feather. Each of those filaments represents a teaching that we gather as we travel. Each teaching helps us to become whole. There are teachings about relationships, work, community, well-being, honesty, truth and principles meant to form the foundation of our days. Everything that we do as a matter of course in our life has the potential for teaching if we choose to look. So like that feather we are a sum of all the teachings we gather in our life.

One side is always wider than the other. That's because some teachings are more vital than others but they are all necessary in order for the eagle and we humans to achieve grace, to soar higher, to see further. Then he said if I turned the feather over I would see that it becomes its opposite. That's because there are stronger and weaker teachings that come to us through stronger or weaker choices. Our life becomes whole when we can see the teachings that come to us through the power of choice.

The eagle has the gift of vision. The feathers enable him to achieve the height necessary see a long way. When we reflect on our lives we come to recognize the effect of teachings, even those we perhaps didn't recognize as such when they were happening for us. To be given an eagle feather is to be recognized for having the vision and the courage to live a life based on principle.

My life becomes more when I learn where to look. There are teachings everywhere and the ones I choose to find through the power of strong choice flesh my life out, make it fuller, let me soar. The eagle feathers in our home represent strong choices. They are my daily reminders.

I SPENT YEARS patrolling the margins of things believing that from there I could observe and know. But the truth is I couldn't. And I didn't until I learned to walk into the centre and even deeper—into the very centre of the centre where NOW is. Now is perfect. It's honest and elegant and pure. This moment, this quiet instant of morning, writing in solitude becomes so much more when I know that I have an Earth to plant my feet on, a sky to gaze up at and ponder the Great Mystery and a heart beating blood through the vessel of my body, open to everything, immune to nothing. I can live here. This life beyond the margins.

WHICH HAT TO WEAR?
LIFE CERTAINLY WAS
SIMPLE AS A STEREOTYPE

IT'S GETTING HARDER and harder to be an Indian in this country. Back in the good old days your average Aboriginal could at least depend on existing stereotypes to amble through the rough spots. Nowadays, with Indians going prime time on a regular basis, you really have to work to be recognized as a bona fide Indian.

In those days, prior to the media explosion of the '80s, the general perception of Canada's Indians was that of guttural, welfare-dependent wards of the state with a charming romantic history. In tense social situations all you really needed to do was grunt a little, remain stone-faced and talk about your grandfather.

Either that or you found it necessary to affect the militant perception of the Indian. To fit that particular dimension you needed to sport long braids, turquoise, beaded vests, moccasins and various Aboriginal accoutrement. Your vocabulary needed to be spiced up with at least four derivations of the word "honky" (there were at least a dozen but four is a strong traditional number) and peppered with references to Che Guevara, revolution, broken treaties, the sanctity of the land and, of course, your grandfather. Then there was the Hollywood image. Those of us who wandered into this scenario soon found ourselves considered "hot invitations" to parties hosted by the liberal minded. To be a Hollywood Indian you absolutely needed to look the part. Long braids, cowboy boots, jeans, beaded paraphernalia and jewellery.

It also was essential that you discuss the sun dance, sweat lodges, vision quests, eagle feathers, the meaning of the circle and, of course, your grandfather.

Fitting into one or all of these stereotypes made it relatively easy to wander around the country and be accepted as a genuine Aboriginal. Then enlightenment happened.

For one reason or another, the public began to latch on to the idea of Indians as diverse cultures and our cover was blown forever. Suddenly there were Native politicians on television, artists and playwrights being interviewed on *Morningside*, Native lawyers pressing cases and causes in the Supreme Court, Native teachers, journalists, social workers, doctors and policemen.

With the cultural light switch thrown open, people everywhere discovered Indians. They discovered that there were more than just the Apache, Cherokee, Sioux and Cheyenne. Indians were everywhere. They discovered the Dogrib, Flathead, Saulteaux, Oneida and Ojibway, and when they stumbled upon them they found warm, humble, humorous, kind, politically astute and culturally motivated nations within their own nation.

They discovered there was a history of their country that was never revealed in the history books or school texts. They discovered nations of Canadians who had added much to the fabric and fibre of their homeland and had been credited with none of it. They discovered a missing part of themselves.

And that's what makes it so difficult to be an Indian these days.

When there was just us concerned about us, you only had to identify yourself as either a Treaty Indian or a non-status one. The Métis would gain constitutional recognition in the '80s, as would the Inuit and the Bill C-31 people, and then came the monikers of urban Indian, traditional Indian and the Warrior.

Suddenly you needed to know your heritage, have an encyclopedic knowledge of the land-claims process, speak your language, be able to skin a moose, recite Chief Seattle's address in its entirety, discuss the prohibitive effects of a welfare mentality to the fostering of a culture and quote crucial constitutional passages pertaining to the plight of your people.

Talking about your grandfather just wasn't cutting it anymore.

Sure, you still could score points at parties with references to sweetgrass, hand drums and powwows, but more and more we Indians would find ourselves pressed to digress on residential schools, the fur trade, the relative merits of party politics on Native organizations, fiscal restraint, the OST and its effects on our tax status and comparative analysis of the Mulroney and Trudeau cabinets.

It started to seem like we were required to qualify as Aboriginal—all of which is fine, but there's a certain element within our communities that hungers for the security of relative anonymity.

Because it used to be somewhat comforting to simply grunt, look quizzical and wander away in stone-faced elegance to another corner of the room. Nowadays, they follow you.

It's become downright hip to be up on Indian issues and it's requiring us as Aboriginal people to look more closely at who we are, where we came from and where we want to go. Grandfather, I think, would be proud.

FOR YEARS I FILLED myself with envy, jealousy, greed, false pride and wild narratives spun by my ego. On that diet I was never filled. I was always craving more. Nowadays, I am learning to live the opposite. As much as I can I fill myself with prayer, meditation, calm, giving and receiving love and kindness and moments of stillness. These days I feel filled. I find my Creator in a jazz ballad, a great passage in a book, the wind on my face, a single candle glowing in the morning dark and the assured, directed narrative spun by my heart.

THE TRUE MEANING
OF CHRISTMAS

WHEN I WAS FIVE I got a truck for Christmas. It wasn't any special kind of truck, not like the huge replica trucks around today; it was just a tiny red truck with a blue cab and one wheel missing.

In 1960 such a truck might have cost seventy-five cents. My brothers and sister somehow had scraped together the money, wrapped up the truck in brown paper and laid it under the tree. Christmas morning. It was the only present the four of us shared that year. As the baby of the family, they wanted me to have something at least. We were foster-home kids by then. Separated from our natural family by the Ontario Children's Aid Society, we were together in a group home with about six other kids. Christmas was a tree and a meal shared at one long table apart from the foster family, who ate in another room. That year it was also a small red truck with one wheel missing. I loved that truck. In the deep freeze of a northern Ontario winter I'd be plowing roads, building towns or exploring countries in the snowbanks for hours at a time. And many a morning I'd awaken with the imprint of the fender or the cab of that truck creased into my face. As my siblings headed off to school on the bus I'd be standing at the road with that little red truck cradled under my arm, waving and waving. It was a great Christmas present. My sister Jane often recalled how inseparable that little truck and I were. I never seemed to mind that there was a wheel missing. In that special world of children such things are irrelevant and the fact that only one present was handed out that year, or that there were no greater celebrations than that one crowded dinner table, became irrelevant as well.

I don't remember the worlds that truck and I entered together. I don't recall the mysteries we unravelled, the wonderful strangers we encountered, the adventures we rumbled our way through or the shadowy childhood secrets I shared with it. But as I knelt beside our Christmas tree last week replacing a tumbled ornament, the memory of that little red truck was right there with me.

It came to mean a lot more than Christmas very soon after.

The following spring I was removed from that home and sent away, alone, to live in another foster home. I would not see my family again for almost twenty years. My sister Jane still talks about that last morning. You see, my siblings had been told I was leaving and thought it better to just let it happen rather than inform me beforehand. As she left for school that day I was sitting in the sandbox with my little red truck, building castles. She came, threw her arms around me and silently hugged me for a long, long time.

For twenty years two images stuck with her: The first, the view from the back window of the school bus, of me hunched over in the sandbox busy building something. The second, when the bus returned, of a sandbox deserted except for one little red truck with one wheel missing and the wind already busy burying it in the sand.

When we met again two decades later she came, threw her arms around me and silently hugged me for a long, long time. I think about that little red truck almost every Christmas now . . . That little truck was the best Christmas present I ever received.

Some small, little-boy part of me still sleeps with the love and compassion that went into its purchase . . . It never mattered that this gift was simple, small, perhaps insignificant in comparison to the glitter that's available, or that it came wrapped in a brown paper bag, Scotch-taped and without ribbon. The reason the memory lingers throughout the years is because of the genuine way in which it was offered. And that, for me, is the magic of Christmas. Genuineness and simplicity. I forget that sometimes as I join the hustle and bustle and endure the lengthy lineups. But in the quieter moments it all comes tumbling back. I believe that if we could all connect to that genuineness and simplicity and make it last the whole year through, we'd all be one step closer to heaven. Just as I believe, that for me and my family, that same heaven consists of a great big sandbox where we gather to laugh and play, building castles, adventures and futures with a little red truck with a blue cab and one wheel missing.

I DON'T KNOW that I personally know anything of real weight and consequence. In very real terms, any knowledge or hint of wisdom that I have is borrowed from other people, protocols, ceremonies, teachings and processes. But I do know this: If I commit myself to a rigorous daily practice of spirituality, my life becomes extraordinary. Not in riches or acclaim but in a calm and abiding assurance that I live under the grace of a loving, benevolent and eternal Creator. That spiritual energy guides me to things, events, circumstances and people I could never have found on my own. It is love. And love in my ceremonial way means "you leading me gently back to myself." Thank you Creator of all things, for the gift of this way. Now there is only one thing left to do—repeat what got me this far.

STRIPPING IT DOWN

IN THE CORNER of our yard nearest the gravel road is an old wringer washer. It sits beneath a fir tree with its barrel filled with earth and dirt and sprouting flowers over the rim. Further back, near the front door, an old wagon wheel leans against a pine tree. Both of them hearken back to a simpler time. Rustic, some might say, but for me merely elegant and uncomplicated.

When we came here we had to disassemble everything, strip away the clutter of life. A painting that seemed relevant in a city context suddenly became unnecessary here. Books that marked the footsteps in a cosmopolitan journey were rendered irrelevant by the presence of bears.

It surprised us both, this abrupt introduction to the nature of stuff. It sits on our shelves, rests in our closets, nestles in our corners singing it histories. We come to need that voice. We come to believe that it defines us, gives us definition, offers scope to our living, our being here. But in the end, when you strip it away, it's just stuff.

Oh, there's the usual accepted arrangement of things still. Along with the woodstove in the living room is a television, stereo, computers, furniture and we've held on to the art that retains its original frankness.

It reminds me of my journey back to reclaiming my culture. In the beginning I thought that I needed a conglomeration of stuff to make me an Indian. I thought I had to live my life within an Indian motif, with native art, native books, native music and native fashion. So I collected roomfuls of stuff.

But when I began to attend ceremony and was introduced to genuine traditional teachers I confronted a simplicity that astounded me. Everything in my world needed to be reflective of my identity. The teachers I found were nothing like that. Sometimes it was only the braids in their hair that bore any sense of the stamp of Indian-ness.

I wondered about that. I wondered how you could be authentic without the signature. I wondered how you could be at peace with who you are without the trappings, the statements of being. So I asked.

What I was told changed the way I live my life. I was told to gather a yard of cotton cloth, some ribbon, scissors and a can of tobacco. I was told to make this gathering my mission for one day. Then I was to find a quiet place, somewhere, perhaps, where I felt safe, secure, at peace. I was to go there with my gathered articles and sit.

I was to ask myself why my question was important, why it was necessary that I move to knowledge, and more importantly, how it felt to not carry the answer. Once I'd discerned that, I was to cut a small square of cloth with the scissors, then take a pinch of the tobacco, place it in the cloth and tie it with ribbon.

This small tobacco tie would symbolize my question and my emotional and spiritual need. With it I was to return to my teacher and offer the tobacco and ask for a teaching. Once the tobacco was accepted I could ask my question. It seemed odd, quaint, charming in a folksy kind of way. But I did it.

All true learning requires sacrifice. That's what the tobacco offering taught me in the end. That was the intent of the ritual. That's why elders ask that you make that tobacco offering.

In order to accomplish my quest for understanding I had to sacrifice my time and my money. I had to sacrifice my pride by confronting the truth of my unknowing. In the end I had to sacrifice my humility by asking.

That ceremony stripped away all the stuff that blocked me from myself. In the end it didn't matter how I looked or what I wore. All that mattered was the nature of my question. All that mattered was how I felt about the answer. All that mattered was that I learned that it's the stuff you carry within you that gives you definition, not what you own, collect or cling to.

There is stuff that sings its histories in our lives. It sits in the corners of our being adding resonance to our living. It's the stuff of our passages, our time here, the assembled chorus of our spirit. It's the important stuff, the life altering, life affirming stuff. You have to learn to strip it down in order to hear it, to sacrifice. When you do, you come to learn that what you need is far less than what you have, even what you desire and it frees you. I wouldn't be less Indian by not knowing that—only less human.

WHAT COMES FROM SPIRIT is beyond time, beyond place. It exists in another realm and when I get in touch with it, when I get in touch with my essential self I am transported, altered, changed, empowered and I become less a human being working than a perfect spirit moving. This is powerful. This is truth. This is spiritual.

WHEN I CHOOSE a course of action with my mind I'm mostly reacting to situations based on what's happened before, my usual response. So I live my life reacting to life. But when I choose with my feelings I'm creating an entirely new outcome.

OLD WOMAN: Take me to the mall.

ME: You're kidding right?

OLD WOMAN: No. I love it there.

ME: But it's so not you.

OLD WOMAN: Actually, it's me to a T. I get to wander around looking at all the stuff I'm very happy living without.

That's when I learned the value of window shopping.

WE ARE ALL taken care of. We are all watched over, loved, and sheltered when we ask for it regardless of creed. It is what binds us and makes us a human family. It is our greatest human truth. Let our spirits rise collectively today in celebration and gratitude for the loving Creator / God we feel around us, in us, moving through us. Peace. Be blessed. Be the blessing.

LESSON FROM CEREMONY: Is what I'm choosing moving me closer to Creator or further away? Is what I'm choosing moving me closer to the highest, grandest expression of who I am or further away? Is what I'm choosing moving me closer to my brothers and sisters in my human family or further away? Is what I'm choosing serving me? When I can answer yes to these questions my choosing becomes an act of ceremony and I move closer to my real, essential self.

LUKEWARM TEA IN THE MORNING isn't very satisfying. But it left me to ponder something. I wondered where in my life I'm being lukewarm on things. Like my tea, a tepid involvement with life and living isn't very satisfying. So I started a list. What do I stand for today? It's amazing what comes out. I stand for sobriety. I stand for honesty. I stand for equality. I stand for compassion. I stand for protecting our planet. I stand for forgiveness and I stand for love. There's more, but the point is I don't have time to be lukewarm on the principles I stand for today. They are what guide me to the kind of life I was meant to live. The kind of life I want to live. So make a list, my friends. Let those principles guide you through your day!

SITTING IN THAT indescribable moment when you realize that you weren't looking for anything when Creator dropped something marvellous into your life. Makes it hard to believe in circumstance or luck or magnificent planning on my part. Instead, it keeps me in a pure state of amazement of how when unknown gaps are suddenly filled by grace (me not having to do anything), how secretly and beautifully Creator existed in those gaps all along.

ALWAYS KEEP YOUR BLESSINGS in front of you. It doesn't mean that I inventory everything I have. It means I remain aware of all I've been given. Like breath. Like sight. Like friends, confidants, love, productivity, health, joy and even difficulties so that I might learn to employ other blessings to negotiate my way through them. When I can keep my blessings in front of me, it opens me to awareness of Source and gratitude. I don't have to want anything because I've already been blessed.

MY SPIRITUALITY IS me seeking to be tuned to The Great Mystery that surrounds me. It is me seeking to be opened, to be joined to it, so that it becomes a part of me and I, in turn, become a part of it. It is me seeking to honour the truth of the things that lie beneath the surface of myself, of you, of Creator and Creation, committing to those truths and working toward never allowing them to be invisible to me again. It is me on the shore of the great ocean of truth always seeking a prettier shell or a smoother stone.

OLD ONES CAN SHOW THE WAY TO NEW SELF-UNDERSTANDING

I GREW UP on a hill in Montana. Over the course of four days and four nights, in what has romantically been referred to as a *vision quest*, I confronted the essential nature of myself and stepped forward. Alone on that hill, with nothing more than a blanket and a canteen of water, I was introduced to my place in the world.

The Old One sent me there. I'd come to him again, as I had over the course of the years, confused, angry and willing to do almost anything to change. My marriage had disappeared, my writing well appeared to have dried up and various attempts at relationships with women had ended in turmoil. Most days were spent wishing I was anyone other than myself.

He listened as he always did, smoked his pipe and watched me. After what seemed like an interminable period of silence he described the ritual he was about to send me on.

I was to go out alone and stay within a prescribed circle atop this pine-covered hill.

With no fire and no company I would pray and ask humbly for guidance and for the strength to follow the directions he promised would come. I was given a sacred pipe, some tobacco, sweetgrass and water. Within that circle, which represented the universe, I was to sit and contemplate the questions that churned within me.

He told me that the answers were within me and that they always had been. By confronting myself for four days and four nights, much would be revealed, provided I was willing to look within and to greet the fears as guides to the correct path. A hug, a look I will remember forever for its depth of understanding, a wave and he walked away down that hill.

I'd like to be able to say that I was granted a sweepingly romantic vision like the ones described in novels and movies. I'd like to say that I saw the answers to all the questions in my life. Just as I'd like to say that I walked away from that experience totally healed, fulfilled, directed and pure. But I didn't.

Over the years I made many wrong choices, hurt more people and suffered more at my own hands. Still, something was granted to me then that lives with me today. Something that enabled me to survive the mistakes, grow and heal myself.

As I sat there alone, shivering and prayerful through nights that seemed as full of hidden terrors as they did full of obvious fears, I learned my basic nature. All my life to that point I'd considered fear and vulnerability as weaknesses. Denial was strength and the warrior spirit I sought to project did not include emotional displays or confessions of doubt. But there on that hill I was introduced to the part of myself I'd hidden from.

As the Old One walked me back down the hill he listened as I explained how I'd come to realize that denying my fears and inadequacies was basically a denial of myself. He smiled when I said that the reason I'd been unable to deal honestly with women was because I'd been unable to deal with what I saw as the female of myself.

When I left him the next day to drive back into my life, he gave me two eagle feathers bound together with a deerhide thong and a red ribbon. They were to be both an honour for enduring an ordeal and a reminder that I would always have two sets of gifts within me. The gifts of the father, represented by my male characteristics, and the gifts of the mother, represented by the feminine side of my nature I'd denied, all my life.

The gifts of the father—like independence, aggression and strength—and the gifts of the mother—like nurturing, compassion and humility—needed to work alongside each other if I was to live as a fully functioning human being. This was spiritual, this was traditional, this was Indian. The feathers hang in my living room today as a constant reminder of the true Indian way that I strive to live.

The Old One has departed this reality. He left with grace, dignity and a characteristic lack of fanfare. There is much fear in knowing that my spiritual teacher who enabled me to change my life is no longer within reach. But as I stand on that Montana hilltop he will always be a part of the breeze. He lives as all grandfathers live. He lives in ceremony, in ritual, songs, dances, prayers. He lives in the kindness and dignity we human beings grant to each other in our comings and goings and it is my hope that he will continue to live in these words . . .

Meegwetch, my friend, Meegwetch.

THE WORLD IS CHANGEABLE but the truth stays the same. Life is a whirlwind of change; accidents happen, people get ill, lovers leave, loved ones die, the bottom sometimes falls out of things. But the truth is that we all exist under the hand of grace. That stays consistent. Always. It's believing that through the harder times and acting out from that belief that allows me to experience the whole gamut of life without buckling, regressing, isolating or giving up. My people say that there is a teaching in everything and to follow ceremony is to always look for the teaching. At its core, the universe is light.

I LEARNED TO LISTEN when I was given to understand how much can be heard in silence. I learned to listen when I was given to understand how much remains unspoken beneath the words we say to each other. I learned to listen when I was given to understand how the real stories live in real human moments when nothing is said. I learned to listen when I was given to understand that Creator communicates with me most clearly through feeling and not words.

MY SEARCH FOR A SPIRITUALITY that works in all circumstance has led me to the truth that Creator is a Great Mystery hiding in the open. When I breathe in I draw in the breath of all things; when I exhale I contribute to the breath of all things. I am connected. I am joined to the channel of loving, nurturing energy that joins and sustains all of us. When I come to know that, understand it and believe it, my life becomes the process of keeping that channel open. Creator is hiding there.

THERE'S A DEAFENING SILENCE when warriors fall, an interruption in the universal flow. Those on the edges can only wonder at the silence while those who were a part of the life must, by turn, suffer, remember and move on.

True warriors are rare. They come to our circles anonymously, strengthen, expand and redefine them, asking nothing but the freedom to be heard and the grace to be themselves.

Such warriors know that bravery on display is just the ego doing gymnastics.

True leaders lead by quiet example, the voice of the breeze whose spirit is eternal while the vainglorious lead by loud display, the voice of thunder that rumbles once and fades away.

Death does not separate us from the true warriors. Instead, reflection on their contribution adds to the fabric of our lives and we move forward, secure in the knowledge that our path has been broken by their efforts.

ME: What should I mean when I say "I believe"?

OLD WOMAN: You choose to mean "I give my whole heart to this."

ME: What's the difference?

OLD WOMAN: "Should" is a word that comes from a place where judgment exists. "Choose" comes from a place of love and love has no judgment.

ME: You believe that?

OLD WOMAN: With my whole heart.

ME: Did it change you?

OLD WOMAN: I changed me and my heart came along for the ride.

I became a better person after that . . .

III

THERE ARE NO STRANGERS

CREATOR DOES NOT TELL US who to love. Only that we learn how. Love is spiritual. It comes from the Spirit place. There is no colour there. No gender. No skin, no history, no time, no right, no wrong, no better, no best, and certainly no politics. It is a place of pure love. It is our common home and we all return to it someday. So it is our soul's mission to learn love. Remember that we spring from love and hold your loved ones close.

When you trust your life to Creator and become willing to take the next indicated step all manner of miracles become possible. I remain in slack-jawed wonder at the richness of my life.

THE SOUL OF A NATION is in its people and the spirit of Canada is variegated and sublimely diverse. What makes us strong is our diversity, our differences, but what pulls us together, ties us irrevocably into a common destiny, whole and complete and shining, are the strainings of our very human hearts—the secret wish for a common practical magic.

It exists. It lives. It sails across the sky once a month as fat and round and free as a dream. You need to step out on the land to see it properly. You need to walk away from all that binds you to a city, to a desk, to a job, and stand where the wind can get at you. And when that moon comes up and begins to sail across the sky there will come a point, if you watch it close enough, that the earth will start to move, to race that moon, and you can feel it spin in the heavens.

It doesn't matter who you stand with or where they're from. It happens for both of you. Universal magic inhabiting you, filling you, making you more, joining you, erasing differences.

EACH PATH THAT WE FOLLOW MAKES US WHAT WE ARE TODAY

DID YOU USED TO BE INDIAN? A cousin in my adopted family posed this question when I was about eleven. Of course, everyone at the table erupted into laughter and it was fortuitous timing, since I really had no answer.

At that time I was a round-headed little kid with a brush cut, thick horn-rimmed glasses and an enforced penchant for lime-green trousers, old-man style brogues and white socks. My adopted family was a secure, middle-class, split-level, two-car-and-a-pool-table unit typical of the southern Ontario city where we lived.

So questions about my Indianness at the time were mind-boggling to say the least. Like most Canadians in the mid-1960s, the majority of information I had regarding Indians came from three sources: television, textbooks and movies.

Lost as I was in the non-Native foster-care system, I was as susceptible to their influences as everyone else. Textbooks of the time did little more than relegate Aboriginal people to the status of shadow people in the canoes of the explorers. There were no in-depth investigations of their societal structures, cultures or natures. It was as if my people were window dressing for the heroics of the adventurers. Television, of course, was the domain of the Jay Silverheels–type Indian. As Tonto, Silverheels' portrayal of the loyal Indian sidekick enforced the idea of the

Indian as mute follower dependent on Kemo Sabe for direction and a job.

Unfortunately, Kemo Sabes everywhere in North America, particularly those in government, agreed with the metaphor. Movies merely extended the TV image. My people were forever popping up over hillsides. It almost was as if Indians never rode through the bottom of valleys. For a while I grew up believing I had to pop up over the side of a hill when I arrived anywhere. I also was supposed to be brutal, guttural, susceptible to dangers of firewater and be from either the Cheyenne, Cherokee, Sioux or Apache nations.

Apparently, movie-makers back then never had heard of the Dogrib, Sarcee, Flathead, Choctaw or Ojibway.

So my cousin's question caught me by surprise. I'd never been any of the things that my three primary sources outlined for me and my world at the time was an all-white one. For all I knew, this was what I was and the truth of my life was, indeed, that I used to be an Indian.

Coming around to rediscovering my roots, reconnecting to my cultural base and redefining myself as an Aboriginal person has been the work of some twenty years now. The forced removal from my family in 1959 brought much pain and confusion in later years, just as the reconnection has brought much joy. For a number of years I wandered around believing that I needed to find the ONE true Indian reality. I assumed that being an Aboriginal person meant that I needed to fit that one tight little slot that every other Native Canadian just naturally slid into when they were raised within their community.

There was a period when I depended on the outward manifestations to define my Indianness. Long braids, lots of turquoise jewellery, fringed vests, beaded jackets, moccasins, and an outrageously militant attitude were my way of expressing my identity. It also was a means of masking my insecurity. Another period of my life was devoted to the urban professional image of the Indian. Silk suits, wide-brimmed hats, attaché case, big salary, lots of boards and committees, short hair and an outrageously militant attitude became another way of expressing my ethnicity. It, too, was a way of masking my insecurity.

Then there was the devil-may-care, drugged, alcoholic, I-never-got-a-break-from-society reality I lived for a number of years. Sleeping under bridges isn't exactly a traditional way of being in harmony with nature and drunken railing and ranting isn't prayer, but it's probably the best way of masking insecurity.

Each of these realities has lent itself to the Aboriginal man I am these days. In each of them there has been something worth keeping, something essential that needed to be carried onward. And I've come to realize that I really did "used to be an Indian," because it's evolution that makes us what we are. Whether we're Aboriginal or not, it's the paths we have trod that enable us to walk our own way today. The culturally alienated, incarcerated, alcoholic, drug-addicted, militant Indian I used to be has enabled me to become the traditionally minded Native man I am today. Each of these realities has helped me ease into the one reality that's important now. Today. Did I used to be an Indian? You bet. Lots of them.

UNDER A RAVAGED SKY all the busted dreams and anguish culled from a lifetime of travelling and running the gamut of human experience draw the wanderer to the heart of another bleak and dire city. Settled in the smoke and noise he contemplates. He wonders. He probes his minstrel heart. He feels the articulation of things rise in him like a wave that breaks over the coast of his being and he begins to speak, to rage, to pray, to attempt to cauterize the seeping wounds of too much, too often, for too long. This is dark. This is anguish. This is truth. But in the end, it becomes forgiveness. It becomes a statement of being. Our being. We humans. We who are graced with the knowledge at our core that our deepest, darkest nights will always pass and we will find peace in the heart of loss and uncertainty. It's about enduring long enough.

OPEN SHARING
OF KNOWLEDGE
BRIDGES GAPS

IT'S AMAZING SOMETIMES how it works. The Old One
had told me a few years back when I was visiting almost
weekly, reintroducing myself to the traditional, spiritual and
philosophical ways of my people, that there would be times when
I would be asked to give it back. I had no idea what he meant, but
these days it's displayed to me regularly.

Walking past a steelyard last week a small group of boys
were roughhousing. The victim of their bullying was a young
Native boy with long braids. They were laughing, pushing and
teasing in the way all kids do once the pack instinct sets in.
However, it was obvious that the young Indian boy wasn't having
a very good time.

When he started crying they threw a few more jibes his way
and left, laughing at some kind of victory. He was still sniffling
when I approached him.

After making sure he was uninjured and after polishing off
a Coke at the nearby 7-Eleven, he started telling me about the
ruckus. The kids were roughing him up over his hair. They called
him a little girl, squaw, sissy and told him he wasn't really an
Indian since he and his mother were living in town.

His mother had made him wear his hair braided ever since
he was a toddler and he'd got used to it being that way. The only
explanation he'd ever received about it all was "because that's the

way Indian men wear their hair." He was crying because he felt his hair was the root of his troubles in the playground and he didn't understand why he had to wear it that way.

So I explained to him what the Old One had told me.

The process of braiding hair is like a prayer, he said. Each of the three strands in a single braid represents many things. In one instance they might represent faith, honesty and kindness. In another they might be mind, body and spirit, or love, respect and tolerance. The important thing, he explained, was that each strand be taken as representative of one essential human quality.

As the men, or the women, braided their hair they concentrated or meditated on those three qualities. Once the braid was completed the process was repeated on the other side.

Then as they walked through their day they had visible daily reminders of the human qualities they needed to carry through life with them.

The Old One said they had at least about twenty minutes out of their day when they focused themselves entirely on spiritual principles. In this way, the people they came in contact with were the direct beneficiaries of that inward process. So braids, he said, reflected the true nature of Aboriginal people.

They reflected a people who were humble enough to ask the Creator for help and guidance on a daily basis. They reflected truly human qualities within the people themselves: ideals they sought to live by. And they reflected a deep and abiding concern for the planet, for life, their people and themselves.

Each time you braid your hair, he told me, you become another in a long line of spiritually based people and your prayer joins the countless others that have been offered up to the Creator since time began. You become a part of a rich and vibrant tradition.

As the young boy listened I could see the same things going on in his face that must have gone on in my own. Suddenly, a braid became so much more than a hairstyle or a cultural signature. It became a connection to something internal as well as external—a signpost to identity, tradition and self-esteem. The words Indian, Native and Aboriginal took on new meaning and new impact.

As he walked away smiling, I knew from my own experience that he would handle the jibes and insults in the playground in new, stronger ways, just as I had in the larger adult world. And that's the thing of it. When the Old One told me that there would come a time when I would have to give it all back, he meant the process of sharing what I had learned and gained. This small boy in the playground was just one example. When Aboriginal peoples in Canada talk about the necessity for healing in order to build stronger communities and better relations with outside people and governments, it implies a responsibility. That responsibility is sharing. An open, fearless sharing of those things that define us mentally, spiritually and philosophically. Just as that small boy became bigger through the passing on of knowledge, so too can Canadian society become wider through an intimate understanding of Aboriginal reality. As the Old One knew, healing has to come from the inside. By bringing politics down to the people, by explaining Aboriginal issues in the language of the living room by way of personal experience, bridges can be built between peoples.

In this way, the Old One said, life itself becomes a prayer.

CREATOR DOES NOT ASK US to kill because of religion. She asks us to live in the cause of spirit. Loving kindness. Kindle it today. Love your neighbours as yourselves. Darkness cannot abide the light.

UPSIDE DOWN AND BACKWARDS

I WRITE IN THE DIMNESS of morning. Outside the world is a shape-shifter. Light eases things back into definition, their boundaries called from shadow, hardening, forming, beginning to hold again and the land shrugs itself into wakefulness. Purple moving upward into pearl grey.

It's good to be up and working at this time. I can feel the power of life and light around me and as the letters form upon the screen, race each other to the sudden halt of punctuation, I understand where this need to write comes from. It comes from this palpable mystery. This first light breaking over everything, altering things, arranging them, setting them down into patterns again and tucking shadow back into folds behind the trees. It comes from the need of communion, of joining with that Great Mystery, that force, that energy.

I always wanted to write. There isn't a time I can recall when I didn't carry the desire to frame things, order things upon a page, sort them out, make sense of them. But in the beginning, learning to write was a test, a challenge, an ordeal.

I was the only Indian boy in a mill town school in northern Ontario in the early 1960s. It was a different world then, harder maybe, colder and the idea of Indians was set like concrete, particularly in the parochial, working class confines of a saw mill town two hundred miles from nowhere.

The school was set between the railroad tracks and the pipeline in a hollow between hills above the mill. We sat with the thick sulfur smell coming through the windows and the spume of the stacks on the horizon above the trees. In the classroom I was ignored, set down near the back and never called upon for anything.

They said I was slow, a difficult learner, far too quiet for a kid and lethargic. They said I hadn't much hope for a future and after they held me back a year they just let me be. But I wanted to learn. I was hungry for it and I went to school every day eager and excited about the things we were given to learn.

But I couldn't see. No one had spent enough time with me to learn that. The reason I was slow to pick things up was because I could never see the board. Even at the front of the room where they put me so they could keep a better eye on me, I could never discern the writing on the blackboard. Everything I learned I learned by memory, by listening hard to what the teacher said and memorizing it.

When I was adopted in 1965 I was sent to my first big school in a southern Ontario town called Bradford just north of Toronto. There were hundreds of kids in that school and it seemed like I walked in waves of them on my way to school that first day. Walking through those big glass doors was terrifying for me.

I was in Grade 3 and my teacher wanted to introduce me and she asked me to write my name on the blackboard for the other children to read. I went to the board, leaned close to it, squinted and began to write. I heard snickers at the first letter and open laughter when I'd finished.

I'd written my name upside down and backwards. To the rest of my classmates it was odd, strange and hilarious but it was how I'd learned and I felt the weight of their laughter like stones.

Walking back to my seat that day I felt ashamed, stupid and terribly alone.

But I had a teacher that cared. She walked me down to the nurse's station herself and waited while I got my eyes tested. Astigmatism, the nurse told her. Terrible astigmatism. Then she listened closely to me when I explained why my writing was wrongly shaped.

I taught myself to write by squinting back over my shoulder. When we were taught to write in script I wasn't given any teacher attention, wasn't offered any help in forming the letters. So I watched the boy behind me and I mimicked what I saw on my own page. Unfortunately, what I saw was upside down and backwards and that was how I taught myself to write. I could spell everything correctly but it was all skewed.

Well, I got glasses very shortly after that and my world changed. Once I could see what was written on the board my ability to learn accelerated and I graduated Grade 3 with straight A's. Especially in penmanship.

See, for that teacher I wasn't an Indian. I was a student in need. So she took the time to show me how to write properly. Every day, before and after school, she and I sat at a desk and we worked through the primary writing books. I shaped letters time after time after time until I gradually unlearned the awkward process I'd taught myself.

Like life, unlearning something was a lot harder than learning it. I struggled with breaking down my method and at times it seemed I would never get it right. But I persisted with the help and encouragement of that teacher and I learned how to write in the right direction. But I still shape my G's and D's wrong today. I still write them back to front after all this time.

I write on a keyboard these days. But there isn't a time when I set a pen to paper that I don't remember learning how to write and what it took to get me there.

See, there's a story behind every difference. There's a reason we become the people we become and it's having the courage and consideration to hear those stories that allows us to help each other.

Sometimes life turns us upside down and backwards. It's caring that gets us back on our feet again and pointed in the right direction.

OUR DREAMS ARE GATHERED and held sacred by those who believe in us . . . When I left those lonely roads and took the one that led in a long, curving line of years to here, to a home in the mountains where I write, I am surrounded by those who believe in me and my dreams are their dreams. That's where the magic is, all of us together, sweeping the spotlight that shines on our dreams into the humble dustpan of our hearts and holding them sacred for each other.

I SPENT PART of last night tuning guitars after two weeks away. Slowly, carefully, consciously easing each string on five instruments closer to their perfect pitch. I used the same tuner for each one. Then I played some music. It struck me then how if we are tuned to the same standard we are tuned to each other. So if as a human family we are tuned to unity or harmony or love or any spiritual quality the music we produce together becomes grander—just as a guitar played alone is not nearly as majestic as one played in community. One note is a vibration changing a room. A million notes are energy changing a planet.

NATURE OF THE WARRIOR

I ALWAYS WANTED to be a warrior.

From the moment I stumbled from the relative security of the foster-home/adoption system and landed on the streets of the cities it's what I've wanted, because it was there I met my people. Not the primitive, guttural savages of TV, movies and books, but the gentle, humorous, harmonious people I have grown to love. And I wanted to fight for them.

For a time I did. As an angry, rebellious young man I took up arms, fought with allies, occupied offices, and graced jails and institutions because of it. It was part of being a warrior, part of the price of refusing to bend. It was the admission to the pantheon of the Dog Soldier and the natural pose for a protector of the people. I became a warrior.

Through the years I have been gifted with the presence in my life of gentle ones who taught me softer ways, ways that enable me to be here and ways that enrich my life immensely. It's changed. But inside my heart, inside my motivation to write these columns is still the motivation of the warrior. The protection of the people.

So, to stand there at the checkpoint in Kahnawake was incredibly difficult.

The warrior in me wanted to join them. Wanted to abandon the quiet life of the scribe and escalate my involvement. Wanted to abandon all the softer things I have learned and return to the front lines.

But I couldn't.

Leaving the checkpoint I felt helpless, powerless, almost a traitor. The deeper stirrings within me wanted to fight and they wrestled with the newer things I've learned since I last held a gun. Wrestled, wrestled and wrestled until I reached a point where I was almost willing to forsake everything I've come to believe in. Everything that has changed my life.

It's taken some time and much inner struggle to realize a few things, the foremost of which is that I will always be a warrior. Only my front lines have changed. Those front lines are here telling the stories that need to be told and they are just as important as the front lines at Kahnawake or anywhere Native people choose to stand up for their rights.

I had to realize the truth again about something the Old One told me about the nature of the warrior. All the turmoil made me forget, but its resurfacing was my salvation. He said the warrior has two functions.

One, the obvious, is to be prepared at all times to stand up and defend the rights and lives of the people whenever they are threatened.

The second, the subtle, is to be prepared at all times to help the people help themselves, to work with them as well as for them.

He said, to make other people suffer is easy. To inspire anyone to change, grow and heal is far more challenging and requires greater courage, strength and determination. A warrior, therefore, needs to know healing before he knows conflict.

The siege continues at Kahnawake. It will for some time and the warriors there will continue to stand up for the protection of their own. But it is not them that Native people should attempt to emulate, for the real warriors in Indian country are those who quietly seek to implement growth, change and healing through their efforts as doctors, lawyers, teachers, politicians, mothers and fathers. They seldom make the front page and they don't often attract the focus of the nation but they continue to be the protectors.

You don't need a gun to be a warrior. I had to learn that through much personal pain. All you need is a deep, honest and abiding desire to see that the future of your children is blessed with as much security, hope and possibility as Creation will allow. Set your mind, body and spirit to work and make it happen.

That's a warrior—Indian or otherwise.

ME: Does Creator ever give ME any power or do I have to keep asking for it?

OLD WOMAN: She does. She allows you to choose.

ME: But what if I choose wrong?

OLD WOMAN: Choose again. That's your power. Choose what moves you closer to Creator, to your own right path.

ME: What's the teaching then?

OLD WOMAN: You can't fail when you choose with love.

UNLESS YOU'VE
BEEN THERE

UNLESS YOU'VE BEEN THERE you can never really understand. Unless you've travelled the dark and twisted road of substance abuse, the appreciation of what it takes to recover will always be lost upon you. Until you've agonized over a craving that runs so deep and yet remains so subtle, you don't know what it means to be addicted.

It's a curious world. Because the very thing that you need to live is the very thing that kills you. If you don't die physically you erode slowly. Bit by precious bit, you suffer the insidious death of your mental faculties and your spiritual essence. You move from days when you're sure you'll die into days when you wish you would.

Back and forth, back and forth, back and forth. Because there are no ups and downs in that curious world, only a flat, relentless to and fro. Life in the absence of light.

For years I existed in that twilight zone of alcohol and drugs. For years my world was a hollow one and my dreams the tortured dreams of innocence lost in a golden liquid rush. In that world there was only me and therein was the horror because it was really me I wanted to be free of.

[. . .]

For me the answer lay in a pair of brown eyes. A pair of eyes that had seen what I had seen, closed themselves to those things I had closed myself to and cried the same tears over the same hurts, angers and frustrations. A pair of eyes that looked into mine and said, "I understand because I've been there."

I'VE COME TO UNDERSTAND that the pain of a wound or a loss is over as soon as it happens. What follows is the pain of getting well.

TO BE DEPLETED in the pursuit of a grander something is never truly exhausting. Certainly the tiredness is real and daunting but the lingering effects of perhaps helping to change and alter lives for the better and the majestic transcend all that. Today I am depleted. But I am also filled with energy and purpose.

GATHERING

BECOMING A PROFESSIONAL WRITER is a process. I've been at it a long time now and I'm still learning, still working to grasp and use new tools, new approaches. This month will mark the thirty-second year that I've collected a paycheck for writing. In that time I've moved from newspaper to radio to television to novels, memoirs and poetry. Along the way I've learned incredible amounts of things about the world, life, philosophy, and myself. I wouldn't trade this life for anything.

Back when I first started there were no personal computers. We still used typewriters and carbon paper. There was no email and even a fax machine was considered unbelievable technology. We used to glue newspaper pages together. Research was done through books in libraries, archives and museums. To become the writer I am meant learning to negotiate one heck of a lot of changes in a short time.

Becoming a human being is a process too. It takes a lot of work to create a personal history. There's far more to it than just showing up for life every day. There are choices, both profound and banal, that need to be made. There are things to consider. There are numerous directions to take at a moment's notice and there are literally a multitude of people willing to offer opinions, advice, suggestions and judgment.

Just when you think you know, life comes along to show you that you really don't. For instance, when I made it back to my people when I was twenty-four, there wasn't anything I wanted more than to be regarded as a genuine Ojibway. See, I'd been lost for a long time and had no real idea of who I was. Foster homes and adoption into a white middle-class family will do that to you.

So by the time I made it home all I wanted to do was fit in and represent myself as the best Ojibway possible. The people I saw around me at gatherings and powwows and ceremonies made me proud—and I really wanted to reflect that pride. I set out to be the most Native person I could be. But I was terrified of failure.

I thought that being a genuine Ojibway meant that I needed to know how to do certain things. Like hunting and fishing, how to set a gill net, to track a moose, to speak my language and conduct ceremony. I thought it meant doing warrior things in a warrior world—or at least, what was left of it. As a man I thought that I needed to learn manly things expressed, of course, in an Ojibway motif.

But a woman I met set me straight. I was at a traditional camp north of Temiskaming. It was called a cultural survival camp and I took it at its word. I wanted to survive as a cultural person. One morning when the men set out to do some hunting for the evening meal, I asked to go. The oldest men looked at me and refused to take me. I was crushed. I felt defeated and unworthy.

"Come with me," the woman said and led me into the bush. For an hour she sent me hacking through the timber for dry branches I could snap off with my hands or feet. I gathered armloads and trundled them back to camp. It was hot, sweaty work but I still felt useless and unworthy.

But when we got back to camp she told me to look at the old people. She told me to imagine how much they would appreciate a good, blazing fire in the evening's chill. She asked me to imagine how safe it would make them feel. Then, she told me to look at the children. She asked me to imagine how it would feel for them to fill their bellies with meat cooked over the fire I started. She asked me to imagine how happy they would feel.

She told me that gathering wood and lighting a fire was very important work. She said that through it I would learn the biggest thing first. I would learn to care for people. In the end, that's the most warrior-like thing you can do, she told me: to care for the people around you, to place their needs ahead of your own. I've always tried to remember that.

There is always so much more to learn and incorporate into the process of living each day. Staying open to that and being willing to find the big lessons in the smallest of things is what gets you home, really. I've always tried to remember that too.

I REALIZE THAT where I want to go most is nowhere. Not that I don't want to travel because I do. What I mean is in the depths of my morning meditation, when I let go of the world and travel inward, I don't have to leave my couch to be filled, given purpose, to get a glimpse of joy. In that immaculate stillness I touch the Source and am rejuvenated. My soul is tanned. The surf of my spirit unfolds on the coast of my being. I walk my inner geography and am healed.

SKIN

I'M BROWN. It's the second or third thing I notice about myself every morning. The others are that I'm alive and that I have things to get done by the end of the day. Depending on the state of my bladder, the second thing is sometimes shuffled. In any case, by the time I make it to the bathroom and walk by the mirror, the fact that I am brown works its way into my consciousness. Brown. Rich, deep and luxurious. A brown man engaged with the process of living once more time.

I like that. I've grown comfortable in my own skin. It's taken some work but I am definitely at ease being who I am. I thought about this as I lazed on the deck letting the blazing spring sun fall all over me. I wasn't tanning. When you're brown a tan is something that's just redundant. I was simply laying there letting the feeling of rest wash over me. My skin was hot to the touch. I loved the feeling.

Skin is the largest organ in our bodies. Most of us never think of it that way. To us, our skin is the thing we work hard at darkening in the summer, soften with moisturizers in the winter and take care to cover with adequate layers when the cold descends. It's the thing we wash with the most discipline and it's also the thing we recognize when we touch each other.

Strangely, it's also the first thing we recognize when we see each other. I know there are a lot of people around who say, "I never notice the colour of his skin." But the fact that they even have to make that statement is proof that they do. People of colour understand perfectly the notion that all of us enter a room skin first. We can't help it. It is our most obvious attribute.

When I think of skin I think of chasing flyballs on a baseball diamond. I think of how wonderful the sun felt on my arms and face—the skin of them. I think of how alive I felt, and how even in my fifties the sun on my skin energizes me. I think of the elastic feel of it when I was younger and how elegant the lines and wrinkles make me look nowadays.

I think of love when I think about skin. I think about late nights and rolling over and feeling the warm skin of my wife's body against me in our bed. I think how grateful I am. I think how nothing else in the world measures up to that feeling. I think about the way I want to remember that connection—skin first, all of me wrapped around her. I think about how her skin leaves a lingering presence on my own. Skin, I suppose, has a memory.

I think about Elders when I think about skin. I think about the wonderful roadmap of experience and story and teaching that resides in each wrinkle and line on their faces. I think about things like pride and spirituality and cultural strength. I think about their wisdom. I think about the tremendous resource that they are, the free and open university of their experience with a tuition based on the cost of a question.

I think about babies when I think about skin. I think about the smell of them, all soapy and clean and how warmth has a smell too when you concentrate. I think about innocence and immense possibility. When you hold a baby close to you, that's the promise their skin holds. They bless you when you feel their skin. They are the closest beings to Creator and they give you that proximity when you hold them.

I think about touching when I think about skin. I think about the fact that our first physical act when we're born is reaching out—the desire to touch someone. I think how powerful that is. I think about what Creator gave us with that first instinct. Our primal instinct is to reach out, to belong, to be accepted, to be where love exists.

So I think about unity when I think about skin. I think how important it is that we all share that first deliberate act of reaching out. We reach out in innocence, without fear or judgement, to touch another because it's our strongest desire. How great it would be if we could remember that everyday.

SHINNY GAME
MELTED THE ICE

BACK HOME they still call me "the one who went away."

Whenever the Wagamese family gets together, my uncles refer to me that way.

They're old bushmen those uncles of mine and, having never really become comfortable with English, they lean more toward the Ojibway when talking about family. So, for them, I'll always be "the one who went away."

When I was four I disappeared. I vanished into the maw of the Ontario child welfare system. For twenty years the little family I left behind wondered if I was alive and, if I was, where I was and what I was like. The man who walked back into their lives was vastly different from the fat-cheeked little boy who ran so carelessly through the bush.

It was hardest on my brother. My brother Charles, older, quieter, more refined than I, could never forget. It was he who, twenty years later, managed to track me down through Children's Aid Society records and bring me back home.

[. . .]

One winter he hosted Christmas for the family. I travelled from out West and the rest of the Wagamese clan headed from Ontario to Charles's home in Saskatoon, where he was a teacher in a Native cultural survival school.

I arrived a few days before the rest and we had a chance to spend hours and hours together. One morning stands out through the years.

It had snowed the night before and we were out early, standing in the frosty morning air, skates and sticks in hands, staring at the drifts that covered the neighbourhood rink. It was apparent that industry alone would enable us to skate, so we dug into the task of clearing the rink.

Once it was finished, breath coming in thick clouds from our lungs, we still had the energy to race each other getting into our gear. This would be the first time we'd ever skated with each other, despite several long discussion about our mutual love of hockey. I was twenty-six and Charles was twenty-nine.

At first it was tentative. Our passes were soft, unchallenging and our strides loose, casual, smooth. We didn't talk much except to mutter the usual low, appreciative like "nice," "good one," "great shot," perhaps the odd *ooh* and *ahh* at something especially well done.

Nowadays I realize how very much it was like the development of our brotherhood. Then someone—I don't recall which one of us it was—added a little hip as they swiped the puck from the other's stick. Soon the game became a frantic chase complete with bone-jarring checks, elbows, trips and over-the-shoulder taunts as we whirled around and around the rink, each other and the unspoken effects of twenty years.

We must have kept it up for hours. Finally, we collapsed in a sweaty, exhausted heap at the blue line, arms slapped around each other in what was arguably a clean check, sticks strewn across the ice and the puck a forgotten thing tucked away in the corner of the net.

We lay there for a long, long time laughing through our laboured breathing, staring away across the universe. Brothers.

Friends and playmates joined by something far deeper than a simple game of shinny. This was blood, rekindled, and renewed by the enthusiasm of a pair of boys disguised as men.

Neither of us cared what passers-by might think of a pair of Native men hugging on the ice. Neither of us cared that the tears streaming down our cheeks might freeze, or that we'd have to walk home in wet blue jeans. All that mattered was the disappeared years had finally melted down forever into this one hug between brothers who never had the chance to age together.

They call me "the one who went away." My family and I have had to work very hard at repairing the damage caused by the Children's Aid decision of 1959. A lot of Native families have. But the one who went away is home and those years have become a foundation for our future.

I believe we become immortal through the process of learning to love the ones with whom we share this planet. I believe that in the heart of everyone who takes the time to look, there's something like that rink where we've chased each other's dreams and lives around, only to collapse in the tears and laughter that will echo forever across the universe.

And in this, we are all Indians.

FROM MY WINDOW I watch the sure and elegant creep
of the sun across the pine pocked flank of the mountain.
Beneath it the mercury platter of the lake and the
undulation of the land dancing down to meet it at the reeds
where the red-winged black birds sing. The sky is a bowl the
colour of old denim. Why do we gaze at sights like this in
such awe and wonder yet never take the time to see what
miracles we ourselves are? We are that, you know. Miracles
of Creation. Each of us. We are pieces of the sky dancing.

IV

WE ARE ALL STORY

REJOICE. AN ODD WORD that literally means "to experience joy again." That should be our daily mission. To experience joy again. Sure there's stuff that needs doing, stuff to wade through and stuff to fix but there's also the joy of small things: a hug, a conversation, playing a song all ragged and rough on an instrument, walking on the land, listening to great music or enjoying silence and a cup of tea. Rejoice. Fill yourself again.

SPIRITUALITY ISN'T SIMPLY spectacular. It's spectacularly simple. It means whatever moves your spirit. Not your mind. Your spirit. Your mind is not the seat of you. Your soul is. Your spirit. Finding, approaching and engaging with whatever moves your spirit is being spiritual. Music, books, film, art, theatre, dance, a bird skimming a straight line through the air, a sunrise, a breeze, the smell of rain, a quiet conversation, a hug. It's spectacularly simple. If it moves your spirit, it moves you closer to your true, essential self—and so, closer to Creator.

EACH OF US has an essential rhythm: our heartbeat. Each of us has an essential sound: our breath. Each of us has an essential yearning: to belong. Music allows me to connect to life, living, people and Creator, especially when it hits me in the feet, the hips and the rump and I dance in joy of that. We're all the same. Born to celebrate the music of creation and to learn to join in the cosmic dance going on all around us.

NINE VOLT HEART

"He who hears music, feels his solitude peopled at once."
—ROBERT BROWNING

THE FULL MOON throws everything into hazy, bluish light. It's mid-September and in the darkness I can hear the scuttle of deer amid the leaves and sere grasses brought on by an unusual heat that's blanketed us for weeks. There are coyotes on the ridge. They yip at the stark blind man's eye of the moon while the heavy flap of an owl hunting voles throws a skimming shadow across the deck. The lake is a quicksilver sheen. I'm standing at the window unable to sleep. My wife lays curled and dreaming in our bed, the dog nestled in a ball between her feet. Everything is silent now. Even the coyotes surrender their voices to the power of the soft, overwhelming fall of it. Against the sky the trees poke crooked fingers upward and begin to sway in the breeze that eases through the gap, the belly of the mountains that hold the lake that reflects the sky that glimmers with stars that hold the promise of distant worlds that draw my thoughts to this window, this night, this song everywhere descending.

I hear music. Ambient. Quavering. Shimmering in a frail note where the breeze rustles petals busy losing themselves in the long, slow fall into autumn. There are semitones and halftones, rising and falling like the exhalations of my breath at this window overlooking this stretch of ground that is my home. This mountainside where we find ourselves surrounded by the symphonic splendour of Earth, sky and universe. It touches us. It fills us. It is the singular constant of our days and the lull we drift into sleep upon on nights like this, suspended like a perfect fifth in the harmony our lives have ordered themselves into.

There's the dark bulk of a bear scouring saskatoons from the bushes set beside the gravel road. He's been around for weeks too. There's the scent of winter that drives him to pack on the fat he'll need for the long, frigid months to come. Even the loons have altered their call to reflect the taste of cold hung over the reeds. Seasons shifting. Even with the rampant heat there are signs of it. You can hear it if you concentrate enough. *Crackle. Snap. Swish.* Everything turning downward from supple to rasp, from summer's lushness to a frowzy, autumnal sigh. It too has its song.

I come to the window on the nights I can't sleep to drink in the view and to listen for the notes of the song written into everything. I slip out of bed, careful not to wake my wife, and pad carefully into the living room to stand at the window, gaze out at the land and the universe hung with stars and listen. Just listen. When I hear it I close my eyes. I breathe it into me. I feel sublime connection to a music that is pure and primal, elegiac and soaring, spiritual and rousing all at the same time. It brings me peace. It has for years now. There is a quality of music that sits in the cleft of mountains, augmented and stirred by the hands of the wind into shapes and textures and tones, to be sent in slips and shards that ride on shifting shadow and the flow of light, to reside in the chest of a listener that is unlike anything ever heard anywhere before. It's like the effect of hearing the adagio from Dvořák's cello concerto for the first time increased a thousandfold. It's the first blue vibratoless note of Miles Davis's trumpet hitting you square in the heart multiplied by fifty. It's like the first encounter of Nina Simone singing "I Put a Spell on

You" increased by a couple dozen. It's the sprawl of Lee Dorsey's southern swampy R&B, Dock Boggs's woeful Appalachian angst, Anita O'Day's fluid Jerome Kern balladry, Richard Thompson's stinging, agile guitar and the holy rumble of Charles Mingus's bass shaken, stirred and poured upon your soul. Transformative. Transcendent. Timeless.

For as long as I can remember I have heard music in the night. For as long as I can remember I have sought its solace, its shelter, its calm, just as I have sought its resonant jubilation, its rowdy gin-soaked soul, its effusive glee, its hand-clapping, rump-rolling, foot-stomping, mind-bending, heart-thumping, good-timing, blues-shouting, wailing, roaring, cursing, praising, guttural, lyrical, eloquent, elegant diction of experience raised up in hymns to the silences that live in each of us. These moments at the window reconnect me to the heart of all the music I ever heard, to its elemental core and its pervasive, eternal promise. To people our solitude. To make us more. To allow us the grace to continue. I have heard that promise for a long time now. I have lived with it for over fifty years.

It lives in the recollection of a night when I was nine. I'd been adopted and moved out of the bushland of northern Ontario near Kenora to the flat and treeless farmland of the Holland Marsh area of Bradford, Ontario. I was an Ojibway kid and I'd been in foster care from before I could remember. I'd gone into my last foster home the year I turned five. It was all I'd known. Now suddenly I was adopted. No one took the time to tell me what that meant. No one took the time to tell me that I was moving a thousand miles away from everything I recognized. No one told me that my name would change or that I would have an immediate mother and an immediate father and instantaneous brothers. The beginnings of a Shake'n Bake life. All that I heard was that I was going to "a new home." For me it just meant uprooting. It just meant more loneliness.

There were rules to follow in my new home. Hard rules. Rules that drew lines across every facet of day-to-day living and to breach those lines meant that I was bad or stupid or careless or irresponsible. My new father was a policeman and the home was run in the no-nonsense, black-and-white precision of a career cop's world. Chores were assigned and inspected. Rooms and clothes and shoes were expected to be shipshape and tidy at all times. Children were expected to be seen and not heard. For me, at nine and unused to being given any attention or function in the homes I lived in, such scrutiny was a frightening thing. I was terrified of not measuring up. I was worried that if I didn't make the grade in this new home that I would be sent somewhere else even stranger, harder, and lonelier. Being so afraid to mess up meant that ultimately, I did.

The overriding philosophy in my new home was that if you spared the rod you spoiled the child. In other words, proper child rearing demanded that I be strapped and beaten for infractions. That's what mistakes were called. Infractions. What they didn't know, because the social workers in charge of my file had failed to tell them, was that I had been beaten, abused and terrorized in the years I was with my biological family. Physical and emotional abuses were triggers for the trauma that I still carried around in my body and my psyche. Being belittled for failure and then hit were the last things I needed. When it happened and my skin was broken for the first time since the original trauma, I was desolate and terribly afraid. I wanted to flee.

The second element of the "spare the rod, spoil the child" philosophy was banishment. Infractions of the rules meant that I wasn't fit to be seen by anyone and I was sent off alone to my room until sufficient time had passed to make me suitable to be spoken to again. It was always an arbitrary and harsh assessment process. So I sat beaten and alone as filled with desperation as I had ever been and not knowing what to do to comfort myself. I was tragically and utterly alone.

That's when the magic happened.

I'd been given a small blue transistor radio that ran on a nine volt battery. I huddled under my blankets with the earplug in, twirling the dial slowly to find a station. In southern Ontario, forty miles out of Toronto, there were a lot of stations. I slipped passed commercials and abrasive-sounding music searching for a thing I didn't know existed, something to soothe the clamour in my head and in my heart. I was hurt, shamed and frightened. Beneath that all I was bloody angry. I spun that dial slowly. I closed my eyes. Then, suddenly there was the sound of a voice and guitar in the darkness. It was a simple, unadorned song with a plaintive voice overtop of it. It was the sound of desperation, loneliness and hope all at the same time.

> I been 'buked and I been scorned
> I been 'buked and I been scorned, children
> I been 'buked and I been scorned
> Travellin' this world all alone

The woman singing understood exactly how I felt. She sang to me. I let that voice and that guitar fill me, hoping against hope that no one would come in and discover that I had found a way out and take the radio away. I listened with every fibre of my being, and when the song faded and the announcer told me that it was woman named Odetta singing a song called "Buked and Scorned," I vowed that I would never forget it. I never did.

I had no idea of the historical significance of the song. I would find that out later in a library. All I knew was that it seeped into me and soothed the ache I carried. The celebration of faith calmed me. The realization that we are all being watched over gave me hope. That tiny blue radio became my best and most loyal friend. Every time I was given allowance money, I made sure that the first thing I bought was another nine volt. Then I saved for a good pair of earphones to replace the one plug I had. When bedtime came and I was sure no one would know I slipped away into my nine volt universe in search of more music like Odetta's, something to soothe the clamour.

I made more infractions. I got more punishment. I endured more beatings, strapping and abuse. I spent more time banished. But I was never alone. In my secret nine volt world I found the glories of recorded music, a galaxy of words, voices, melodies and tunes that made my sad little world more habitable. I found textures and tones and colours that added to the bleak and drab nature of my existence.

I did have a new home. It lay in the magic realm of recorded music and I went there religiously. I knelt at the altar of Ray Charles, Duke Ellington, J.B. Lenoir, Helen Merrill, Roscoe Holcomb, Connie Smith, and Bob Dylan and hundreds of other stops in a long sonic pilgrimage. I gave it my heart and it gave me one back—a nine volt heart beating against the vagaries and bruising and on into this life I live at fifty-six. A life of love and comfort, shelter, security and community, creativity and home where the wind brings songs in an upper register riding on beams of moonlight at a window overlooking a lake tucked between mountains nestled under the great bowl of a universe, expanding, growing, evolving with the music of the ages . . .

THROUGH IT ALL I open myself to the world and let the light flow in. I am unbound and singing, glad of this day and open to what flows to me.

I LOVE ACOUSTIC GUITARS for the same reason I love people. Every acoustic guitar is hollow at its centre, so that you come to love a guitar for the nature of the song that springs from it, for the rich, fullness it creates. You and I are like instruments. Life hollows us out. How we nurture that hollowness is how we create the song we present to the world. Because hollow is not empty when the soul learns to sing. It's full and these days I'm learning to hear your fullness at the same time I'm learning to express mine.

WE ALL HAVE STORIES within us. Sometimes we hold them gingerly, sometimes desperately, sometimes as gently as an infant. It is only by sharing our stories, by being strong enough to take a risk—both in the telling and in the asking—that we make it possible to know, recognize and understand each other.

I DON'T KNOW how many times people have asked me how to start a novel or a short story or a poem. I'd love to be able to write something, they say, but I never have the time. Usually they say this while watching television or waiting for something to happen. If we all got ourselves to a desk or a work bench or an easel and devoted one hour of every day to bringing something to life we could change everything. It's all about energy, you see and the more creative energy going out means a lot more things become possible. You don't have to be a genius, a master or even make money. The idea is to create. The idea is to become the creator you already are and to add to the creative energy of the planet. When we do that we shape something marvellous . . .

SOMEONE ASKED ME some time ago, "How do you find your life's purpose?" It's taken a while to really process that question. I found it for myself, as I always do, in stillness, in quiet, in solitude. For me (I carry no universal answer) I have to find my joy first—what really moves my spirit. Once I find my joy I am led to my passion—the daily articulation of joy. Then, through a kinetic and passionate interaction with the world I am led to my purpose. The secret lies in joy. When it begins there, my purpose doesn't become a job, a title, a destination; it becomes what it was always meant to become—the sure, calm, daily expression of who I really am.

COWICHAN

IT'S A CALM DAY on Cowichan Bay. The air is so still that the water is like a mirror. Fishing boats line the wharf and they seem to hover in mid-air. The reflection of the island a mile offshore is its perfect twin. The world is glass and there is a feeling here that time does not exist. The smell of saltwater, fish, rope, marine oil, and gas transports you to a simpler time. Wayfarers and mariners. Here they still exist.

[. . .]

It's a fisherman's world that I know nothing of. The boats that sit packed tightly around the wharf are mysterious things. They are oddly shaped to my eye: ungainly and seemingly unsuited for days and weeks on the sea. I've never been an intertidal person. The sights and smells and look of this place inspire the storyteller in me and I look at it all with a hunger to know it.

I'm here to tell stories at a national conference. What fuels me the most when I do these events are mornings like this one. Mornings when I see the world as though for the very first time. It's then I realize again that everything around me has a story. Everything around me has a vital energy that fills me, excites me, connects me to it all. I feel empowered and curious.

That's the wonderful thing about the world and about this country. When you think you know something of it, when you think you understand it and heck, can even glean your own special place in it, the world has the power to upset all that. It has the power to reintroduce you to itself and teach you things about yourself you never knew before. It's always had that power and I hope it always will.

Looking out this window at a world that holds more secrets, I feel those stories all around me. The seabirds, the wharf, the loops and coils of rope, the rugged shore of the nearby island; they all contain stories within themselves. When I close my eyes I can feel them.

There's no special magic to this. You don't have to be a storyteller to glean that. Instead, you just have to be open to the world, to want to fill yourself with it, to want the experience of being somewhere lead you to ask questions and be patient enough for the answers to come.

That's how our traditional storytellers found the motivation to create. They opened themselves to the world and the world gave them story. It still operates the same way. Stories are as close as an open window or a walk through an unknown territory. They wait for you. They want to be told. All that it takes to gather them is the acceptance of the notion that everything exists as story.

As a writer I have come to believe in that. I tend to look at things a lot longer than most people I know. I can study something for hours, intent on discovering what it has to tell me. There's always something. That something usually finds its way into a story at some time or another. What happens for me is that I remain curious about the world and I retain the power of the innocence that comes from a feeling of wonder.

The stories I tell to the people at the conference will include this vision across Cowichan Bay. There's the essence of Canada here. The country revealing another spectacular part of itself to me in images, shapes and sounds foreign to me. The people I spoke to in the museum, on the wharf, in the diner and the quirky shops all add substance to the stories I will tell.

For every story I shape and gather about this country, there is an immense payoff. I become more. The idea of Canada fills me. I can transcend issues. I learn to see the country and my place in it as the articulation of a great story.

I am a part of that story. It's a thrilling prospect each time I revisit it.

WORDS ARE ALL AROUND US. It follows that stories are all around us too. Because I have ears I hear them. When my eyes are open I can see them. With my heart receptive I can feel them. Staying conscious and connected to the world means that stories come to me by taste and smell and wonderfully, magically sometimes, on the pure wings of my imagination when I keep all my other senses open.

LEARNING OJIBWAY

I WAS TWENTY-FOUR when the first Ojibway word rolled off my tongue. It felt all round and rolling, not like the spiky sound of English with all those hard-edged consonants. When I said it aloud, I felt like I'd really truly spoken for the first time in my life.

I was a toddler when I was removed from my family and if I spoke Ojibway at all then, it was baby talk and the language never had a chance to sit in me and grow. English became my prime language and even though I developed an ease and facility with it, there was always something lacking. It never really quite felt real, valid even. It was like a hazy memory that never quite reaches clarity and that leaves you puzzled whenever it arises.

When that first Ojibway word floated out from between my teeth, I understood. You see, that first word opened the door to my culture. When I spoke it I stepped over the threshold into an entirely new way of understanding myself and my place in the world. Until then I had been almost like a guest in my own life, standing around waiting for someone or something to explain things for me. That one word made me an inhabitant.

It was *peendigaen*. Come in. *Peendigaen*, spoken with an outstretched hand and a rolling of the wrist. Beckoning. Come in. Welcome. This is where you belong. I had never encountered an English word that had that resonance—one that could change things so completely.

It was awkward at first. There's a softness to the language that's off-putting when you first begin to speak it. It's almost as if timelessness had a vocabulary. With each enunciation the word gained strength, clarity and I got the feeling that I was speaking a language that had existed for longer than any the world has known. This one had never been adapted to become other languages like English had evolved from Germanic tongues.

Instead, the feeling of Ojibway in my throat was permanence. I stood on ground I had never encountered before, an unknown territory whose sweep was compelling and uplifting and full. *Peendigaen*. Come in. And I walked fully into the world of my people for the first time.

After that I learned more words. Then I struggled to put whole sentences together. I made a lot of mistakes. I was used to the English process of talk and I created sentences that were mispronounced and wrong. People laughed when they heard me and I understood what cultural embarrassment could feel like. It made me feel like quitting, like English could spare me the laughter of my people.

Then I heard a wise woman talk at a conference. She spoke of being removed from her culture, unplugged from it, disconnected and set aside like an old toaster. But she was always a toaster and the day came when someone plugged her back in and the electricity flowed. She became functional again—and the tool of her reawakening was her language.

She spoke of the struggle to relearn her talk. She spoke of the same embarrassment I felt and the feeling of being an oddity amongst her own. She spoke of the difficulty in getting past the cultural shame and reaching out for her talk with every fiber of her being. And she spoke of the warm wash of the language on the hurts she'd carried all her life, how the soft roll of the talk was like a balm for her spirit.

Then she spoke of prayer.

Praying in her language was like having the ear of Creator for the first time. She felt heard and blessed and healed. It wasn't much, she said. Just a few words of gratitude like prayers should be but the words went outward from her and became a part of the whole, a portion of the great sacred breath of Creation again. She understood then, she said, that our talk is sacred and to speak it is the way we reconnect to our sacredness.

We owe it to others to pass it on. That was the other thing she said. If we have even one word of our talk, if that's all we know, then we have a responsibility to pass it on to our children and those who have had it removed from them. You learn to speak for them. You learn to speak to function as a tool for someone else's reconnection. I have never forgotten that.

These days I'm far from fluent and I still spend far more time using English but the Ojibway talk sits there in the middle of my chest like a hope and when I use it, in a prayer, in a greeting, in a talk somewhere, I feel the same sensation as I did with that first word at twenty-four—the feeling of being ushered in, of welcome, of familiarity and belonging.

An English word I admire is reclaim. It means to bring back, to return to a proper course. When I learned to speak Ojibway I reclaimed a huge part of myself. It wasn't lost, I always owned it, it was just adrift on the great sea of influence that is the modern world. And like a mariner lost upon foreign seas, I sought a friendly shore to step out upon and learn to walk again. My language became that shore.

I have an Ojibway name now. I introduce myself with it according to our traditional protocols when I speak somewhere. I can ask important questions in my language. I can greet people in the proper manner and I can pray.

For me, *peendigaen*, come in, meant I could express myself as who I was created to be, and that's what this journey is all about—to learn to express yourself as who you were created to be. You don't need to be a native person to understand that, just human.

WITHIN ME ARE TREES. Within me are bird songs, tides, winds, the shift of glaciers. Within me is a child's cry, an old one's whisper, a heart bursting with joy, love, grieving, sorrow, the calmness of prayer and a shout from the rooftops. Within me is life. Within me is wonder. Within is me is the potential and the possibility of everything and anything. But I need to stay connected to life in order for that to occur. When my everyday waking consciousness is tuned to life and not my own self-seeking wants and dreams, I become that consciousness. I become alive again. Today. Every day. How cool is that?

FINDING ARCTURUS

SOMETIMES AT NIGHT, I'll stand outside our cabin in the mountains and lean my head back to look at the stars. Some nights the sky is so clear that looking upward across the heavens you could swear that you were suspended on a bed of stars just beyond your fingertips.

I've always been a star gazer. I was always entranced by them. In the north where I spent the early part of my boyhood, the summer skies were clear and the northern lights often set the horizon ablaze in crackles and snaps of colour.

It was the sheer size of it that awed me. I hadn't read of light years or the rate of expansion of the universe or galactic clouds or even the Milky Way. Instead I was transfixed by the magnitude of something that far exceeded the scope of my one small life. Magic existed in the holes between stars. I could feel it.

When I moved south after I was adopted at nine the sky was lessened by the harsh city lights and the stars seemed further away. It was a curious feeling—being lonely for the sky.

There was a field down the street from where I lived. It was marked with orange plastic flags on wooden stakes for the development to come. But at night, it was wide and open and perfect for looking at stars. I'd sneak out and stand under that magnificent canopy and even though the light of them was dim and there were far fewer than I was used to, the stars eased me some, lightened my burden. It became my favourite place.

One night a man showed me how to find Arcturus. He was a fellow star gazer. He lived down the street from us and even though we didn't know each other's name we knew each other from the field. We always just stood silently in that patch of open and looked at the sky.

The night he showed me how to find Arcturus, the sky was as clear as I'd seen it there. He stood a few feet away with his face pointed up at the sky and asked me if I'd heard of it. When I said I hadn't, he began to talk.

Arcturus is called the Bear Watcher, he said, because it follows the Great Bear constellation around the poles. Arctis is Greek for bear and it's where the word Arctic comes from. As a star Arcturus is 37 light years away from us and the third brightest star in the sky. He told me all that while looking up and away from me and I felt the awe in his words.

He told me to look at the Big Dipper and when I found the star at the end of the handle to hold my arm up in front of my face, bend the three middle fingers of my hand in and put my little finger on that star. Where my thumb sat was Arcturus.

When I did it I smiled. It was the first time the universe became reachable and the idea that the stars were indeed within reach was implanted in me forever. All through the years of my boyhood, whenever I felt particularly lonely I would hold out my arm, fold my fingers, find Arcturus and feel comforted.

What that nameless man gave me that night was wonder. There were secrets everywhere but I could reveal them for myself if I had the desire to search. Soon I was reading everything I could about the universe. I learned about planets and nebulae, quarks and quasars, red giants, blue dwarfs and black holes and I learned Einsteins's assertion that "my sense of god is my sense of wonder at the universe."

Years later when I sat in traditional circles and heard the Elders and the storytellers talk about the sky and its wonders, they weren't foreign ideas. Everyone shares that sense of mystery at the heavens. We just frame it in different ways. Magic exists in the holes between stars. We can feel it.

We all need someone to offer us wonder. We all need someone to share the Great Mystery of the universe, to open it up for us and allow us to see into it, even a fraction. Then, when we discover it for ourselves, we need to offer it to others, no matter how simple or seemingly odd it might be. It's how the world opens up for us. It's how we learn to see possibility in a universe of change.

WRITING IS BEST and strongest when culled from the battles and the glories of everyday life . . . You have to be willing to sacrifice comfort and safety sometimes, in order to get to the heart of things—and you can never lose sight of love and God or Creator or however you identify the source of the mystery all around us. And you have to tell your story to someone—plainly, directly, openly.

SMALL CEREMONIES

I STAND AT THE SINK washing dishes. It's one of the things that I do around our home that always feels like a ceremony. I can get meditative staring out the window at the lake and the mountain behind it and feeling the pull of the land all around me.

It's a centering thing really, and something that's come to be important to me. Right after we eat I get to it, putting things away, squaring things and washing everything up. It's a pleasure that I like to do alone.

There's something special about taking care of things. I wipe the counters and the stove, clean the floor, get the morning's coffee ready and make sure the dog has food and water. They're all very small acts but they mean something big. It's the man taking care of his home.

Sure, it doesn't sound very manly or very warrior-like but it is to me. I can stand and look out the window at the land around me and feel very good. I can feel very productive and engaged in the process of my home. Plus, it spares my wife the effort and there's a satisfaction in turning away from a chore well done and knowing that things are set. It's as essential an act in our scheme of things as chopping wood.

Sometimes, when there are friends around and the house is filled with talk and laughter and energy, I still retreat to the sink to take care of the duty. Oh sure, they volunteer to help and the talk is always good when they do and I enjoy the shared work but a part of me really loves the solitary feel of taking care of things.

There's a tactile pleasure in the feel of soapy water on the wrists and forearms and small joys to be found in the clink of glasses, the clunk of pots and the rattle of utensils.

And it's not just the dishes. I take care of the flower beds, saw and chop and stack the wood, tend to the fire, shovel snow, clean the gutters, vacuum, dust, mop and make sure the trash gets taken to the dump.

Manly? Maybe, maybe not, but I never really think about it. Instead, I go about the process of taking care of my home without gender issues or the feeling of being emasculated or being cast into male slavery. They've just become the things I do and I enjoy them.

Someone said to me once when I described some of the things I do around my home, "That's not a very Native thing to do?" I wondered about that. I wondered whether when they laid out the plan for Native people whether they thought about life in 2012 and beyond. Here in our mountain community there's not a lot of call for trapping, gill netting, hide scraping or even rock painting.

Instead, I took up photography a few years back. Compared to skinning a moose that's not very Indian either. I'm capturing scenes and objects and shadow and light instead of game. I'm developing prints instead of following them. I press a shutter instead of a trigger and the shots I take leave everything I encounter alive and energized. But the act of taking pictures makes me feel empowered, creative and engaged with my life and my world.

Oh, and I learned to play a little piano too. Whoever said that there's nothing black and white about First Nations reality never spent much time learning to play scales on a keyboard. For most Native people a key signature is what you have to do to get into the washroom at the Indian Affairs office. I worked at collage too for a while and loved the feel of working in visual art. Neither of those are very hunter-gatherer kinds of things but it doesn't matter a whit to me.

See, what I've discovered is that when I do something that moves my spirit, when I feel alive when I do it, when it makes me feel good—it becomes an Indian thing to do by virtue of the Indian doing it. I feel creative, productive and human. I feel engaged in the process of discovering my own unique identity and when I do that I become a better man, a better person and better Ojibway in the process.

So I'll keep on doing dishes and cleaning house. I'll keep on doing the things that move my spirit because that's the real working definition of being spiritual. Doing what moves your spirit. When you find those things and do them you discover that you make everything a ceremony replete with all the small joyous rituals that are a part of it. A ceremony isn't necessarily something you go to — it's what you carry in you.

YOUR GREATEST TOOLS are your senses. Sharpen them so you can write specifically about a taste, smell, sound, texture or image. In this way you bring your vision of the world to the reader.

I DON'T WANT to be the kind of writer who can take the sun and turn it into a shining word in your imagination. I want to take a shining word and turn it into the sun for you. Similarly, I don't want to be the kind of person who can take words and describe my feelings. I want to be the kind of person who can take my feelings and turn them into words.

YOU WALK IN the shadow of the mentor for as long as the road leads upward. When it curves downhill then lays itself flat, you both find the walking easier. It's time to go then. Time to gather all the lessons in your own kit bag and wander. Time to marshal all the teachings together in the soft curl of your knuckles and get to work on creating your own sound.

SOME SAY THE VOICE was born in our primal past, in a keening wail warning our band of predators. Some say it rose from mimicking the ululation of the wind across trees or mountaintops or vast plains. Others claim its roots lay in celebration, in the rowdy, bawdy, devil-may-care triumph of the harvest or the summer equinox. The struggle for freedom lent the voice its beginnings, others say. Or as a gift of the act of communion with the great power of the mystery that surrounds us all, in worship, praise and joy. Wherever its source, the voice when raised is a clarion call and when it is pure or ragged or primal, once heard it is never forgotten.

TROUBADOURS TRUDGE THE STREETS and alleyways shining a light into the dark and dingy corners, searching for the scraps of tales that come from there, the shadowed, half formed recounting of dreams eddying in the rain above a gutter, disappearing by degree leaving only a song in the silence of their vanishing. They wander the cities, towns and villages, listening. Always listening to the clamour and the chorus of voices raised on the street corners or in the saloons and pubs and alehouses where hearts are raised like glasses to the ubiquitous song of their hope, their dreams, their celebratory witness to the whim and vagaries of life lived large and full and howling.

EARLY MORNINGS WITH THE SMELL of medicines in the air and perfect quiet calm you come to realize there are certain things you want to do in life from now on—and they're not the things of youthful dreams and fantasies but rather the desire from now on to kiss like there's only one left, look people in the eye like they're the last one on Earth besides you, watch someone special sleeping, run and jump and play whenever you damn well feel like it and tell people exactly what you mean and feel and think—because you come to realize that youthful dreams and fantasies all end up right here in quiet times of the soul when life and living themselves are all you want to cling to and cherish.

SCROLLS

WHEN I VISITED the Kenora Public Library way back in 1960 when I first learned to read, I was amazed. Through the back door where the kids' section was, existed a world of colour, dream and image that captivated me. When they told me I could take as many home as I could carry, I did. Lugging them back passed the mill into Rideout where my foster home sat was thrilling. I couldn't wait to get to my room.

Not much has changed since then. A library card is still my most prized possession. The stacks of the library are where I feel challenged, engaged, motivated and curious. There are always more worlds to explore and inhabit than I have time for. But I'm still on the lookout for something new to fire my imagination or simply aid me in understanding more of what I do know.

As a writer I live in the culture of books. I have for most of my life. When I open another book there is a whole new world for me to enter and inhabit. I've traipsed through a lot of worlds in my time and my real world has been increased by every journey. I never tire of making those journeys. Maybe it's the kid in me that still hungers for the lure of a real good yarn, an adventure, a fantastic experience where all I know of this world is forgotten in the spell of a created one.

But I come from a people whose world was ordered without the need of books. The Ojibway, like all native peoples in Canada, had a literature that was oral. We spoke our books. We talked our teachings. Our storytellers framed the universe for us and we had no need of printed language. Within our stories was all the stuff of great literature; pathos, tragedy, journeys, romance, great battles, heroes, villains, mystery and spiritual secrets.

They say that at one time in our history we set our stories on the skin of birch trees. We etched them there on the bark with the blunt edge of a burnt stick or pigments formed of earth and rock and plant material that has never faded over time. Sacred scrolls holding stories meant to last forever. Books. Unbound but for the leather thong that held them, unprinted but for the hand that shaped the images, unedited but for the protocol of storytelling that guided them.

I only ever saw a birch bark scroll once. The old man laid it out for me on a plank table top in a cabin tucked far away in the bush and traced the line of history with one arthritic finger, telling it in the Old Talk that I didn't understand. But I could translate his eyes.

In those ancient symbols was a world where legends were alive, where an entire belief system was represented in teachings built of principles that were built themselves of rock and leaf and tree, of bird and moose and sky, and Trickster spirits nimble as dreams cajoling my people onto the land, toward themselves, toward him, toward me. Here was an entire world, a cosmology, an enduring set of principles laid down in a time long passed that promised a learning unsurpassed in my experience. Here was the magic that sustained a people.

This is what I understood from the wet glimmer of his eyes. When he looked up at me with one palm laid gently on the skin of that living scroll, there was pride there, honour, respect and understanding of what I came for, what I needed. He was telling me that words cannot exist without feeling. That a text is only as useful as the truth it holds. That dreams and reality are the same world. That what I know is less important than what I desire to know.

So inhabit what you read. Allow it to fill you. Let the intent of the spirit of the story take you where it will. Stories and books are tools of understanding on the journey of coming to know. Pick them up. Carry them. This is what I carried away. This is the message I brought to my own storytelling to here, to this page, stark in its blankness, waiting like me to be imagined, to be filled.

SOURCES

MOST OF THE SHORT MEDITATIONS in this book were written between July 2012 and July 2013 and originally shared via Richard Wagamese's social media accounts. In 2015, Wagamese gathered some of these meditations into a manuscript, part of which was published as *Embers: One Ojibway's Meditations* (Douglas & McIntyre, 2016). Many of the remaining meditations from that manuscript are included in this volume on pages 7, 10, 23, 24, 25, 26, 28, 30, 36, 37, 41, 45, 46, 50, 58, 62, 66, 67, 68, 69, 70, 71, 72, 73, 74, 78, 79, 80, 82, 85, 90, 94, 100, 104, 107, 108, 112, 119, 123, 124, 125, 132, 133, 136, 145, 153, 154, 155, 156, 157 and 158.

Wagamese also kept a Word Press blog titled "World of Wonders" between May 2011 and November 2012, and pages 11, 19, 21, 29, 31, 35, 51, 54, 63, 86, 95, 109, 113, 135, 137, 140, 141, 146, 150, and 159 are excerpts from the blog.

The pieces on pages 3, 6, 8, 15, 18, 38, 42, 47, 55, 59, 75, 81, 87, 91, 101, 105, and 116 are excerpted from *The Terrible Summer* (Warwick Publishing, 1996), a volume that collected Wagamese's columns for the *Calgary Herald* from 1989 through 1991.

Wagamese also left an unfinished collection of essays on music, *Nine Volt Heart*, and the pieces on pages 99, 126, and 149 are excerpts from that unpublished manuscript.

All above material is published with the permission of the estate of Richard Allen Wagamese Gilkinson.

Pages 14 and 134 are excerpted from Richard Wagamese's *One Story, One Song* (Douglas & McIntyre, 2011), reprinted with the permission of the publisher.

ABOUT
RICHARD WAGAMESE

TYLER MEADE PHOTO

RICHARD WAGAMESE's acclaimed, bestselling novels included *Indian Horse* (Douglas & McIntyre, 2012), which was a Canada Reads finalist, winner of the inaugural Burt Award for First Nations, Métis and Inuit Literature, and made into a feature film, and *Starlight* (McClelland & Stewart, 2018). He was also the author of the memoir *For Joshua* (Anchor Canada, 2003), and the essay collections *One Native Life* and *One Story, One Song* (D&M, 2009 and 2011), as well as a collection of personal meditations, *Embers* (Douglas & McIntyre, 2016), which received the Bill Duthie Booksellers' Choice Award, and a book on ceremony, *One Drum* (D&M, 2019). He won numerous awards and recognition for his writing, including the National Aboriginal Achievement Award for Media and Communications, the Canada Council for the Arts Molson Prize, the Canada Reads People's Choice Award, and the Writers' Trust of Canada's Matt Cohen Award. Wagamese died on March 10, 2017, in Kamloops, BC.